Staff Ride Handbook for the Attack on Pearl Harbor, 7 December 1941:
A Study of Defending America

LTC Jeffrey J. Gudmens
and the Staff Ride Team
Combat Studies Institute

Combat Studies Institute Press
Fort Leavenworth, Kansas 66027

Library of Congress Cataloging-in-Publication Data

Gudmens, Jeffrey J., 1960-
Staff ride handbook for the attack on Pearl Harbor, 7 December 1941 : a study of defending America / Jeffrey J. Gudmens and the Staff Ride Team, Combat Studies Institute.
   p. cm.
Includes bibliographical references.
  1. Pearl Harbor (Hawaii), Attack on, 1941. 2. United States—Armed Forces—Organization. 3. Japan—Armed Forces—Organization. 4. Pearl Harbor (Hawaii)—Tours. I. U.S. Army Combined Arms Center. Combat Studies Institute. Staff Ride Team. II. Title.
  D767.92.G84 2005
  940.54'266931—dc22
                  2005025669

Reprinted June 2009

Foreword

The *Pearl Harbor Staff Ride Handbook* is the ninth study in the Combat Studies Institute's (CSI's) Staff Ride Handbook series. LTC Jeffrey Gudmens' handbook on Pearl Harbor allows individuals and organizations to study this battle not only in the context of the Japanese attack but, more importantly, in the context of issues that are relevant to the current global war on terror. In addition to analyzing the actual attack, Gudmens also enables users of this work to examine the problems associated with conducting joint planning and operations between the US Army, the Army Air Forces, and the US Navy. He also provides insights into the problems of a Homeland Security environment in which intelligence operatives from a foreign nation (and potentially even recent immigrants from that foreign nation who are now US citizens) can operate with little hindrance in a free and open democratic society. Additionally, this study provides an opportunity to look at how military commanders and planners prepared for their wartime mission with inadequate resources and equipment. Each of these issues, and others analyzed herein, is as relevant to us today as it was almost 65 years ago. Modern military professionals for whom this handbook was written will find a great deal to ponder and analyze when studying the events leading up to, and including, the attack on Pearl Harbor. They are lessons that we cannot afford to forget. *CSI—The Past is Prologue!*

Timothy R. Reese
Colonel, Armor
Director, Combat Studies Institute

Contents

Page

Foreword i

Figures v

Introduction 1

I. The Militaries 5
    US Organization 5
    Japanese Organization 14
    Ships 18
        Aircraft Carriers 18
            Japanese Aircraft Carriers 19
            American Aircraft Carriers 22
        Battleships 23
            Japanese Battleships 24
            American Battleships 25
        Cruisers 28
        Destroyers 29
        Submarines 30
    Aircraft 32
        Fighters 32
            Japanese Fighter 32
            American Fighters 33
        Bombers 34
            Japanese Bombers 35
            American Bombers 36
    Strategy 38
    Operational 42
    Tactics 43
    Logistics 45

II. Pearl Harbor Campaign Overview 47

III. Suggested Route and Vignettes 63
    Introduction 63
    Stand 1. Japanese Espionage 67
    Stand 2. Homeland Defense 71
    Stand 3. American Intelligence 75
    Stand 4. American Preparations 80

		Page
Stand 5.	"Joint" Defenses	88
Stand 6.	Preparednes and Early Warning	94
Stand 7.	Japanese Air Superiority	99
Stand 8.	Japanese Torpedo Attack	104
Stand 9.	Japanese High-Level Attack	108
Stand 10.	Japanese Second Wave	113
Stand 11.	Aftermath	119

IV. Integration Phase for the Attack on Pearl Harbor 123
V. Support for a Staff Ride to Pearl Harbor 129
Appendix A. Order of Battle, Japanese Forces 131
Appendix B. Order of Battle, US Forces 137
Appendix C. Biographical Sketches 143
Appendix D. Medal of Honor Conferrals for the Attack on
             Pearl Harbor 153
Bibliography 159
About the Author 163

Figures

		Page
1.	US War Department Organization	5
2.	Hawaiian Department Organization	7
3.	US Navy Department Organization	8
4.	US Chief of Naval Operations Organization	9
5.	Pacific Fleet Organization	10
6.	Task Force 1 Organization	11
7.	Task Force 2 Organization	12
8.	Task Force 3 Organization	13
9.	Japanese Government Organization	14
10.	Combined Fleet Organization, 1941	16
11.	Combined Fleet Organization, December 1941	17
12.	HMS *Argus*	18
13.	*Akagi*	19
14.	*Kaga*	20
15.	*Soryu*	20
16.	*Hiryu*	20
17.	*Shokaku*	21
18.	*Zuikaku*	21
19.	USS *Lexington*, CV-2	22
20.	USS *Saratoga*, CV-3	22
21.	USS *Enterprise*, CV-6	23
22.	*Hiei*	24
23.	*Kirishima*	24
24.	USS *Nevada*, BB-36, Nevada Class	25
25.	USS *Oklahoma*, BB-37, Nevada Class	25
26.	USS *Pennsylvania*, BB-38, Pennsylvania Class	26
27.	USS *Arizona*, BB-39, Pennsylvania Class	26
28.	USS *Tennessee*, BB-43, Tennessee Class	26
29.	USS *California*, BB-44, Tennessee Class	27

30. USS *Maryland*, BB-46, Colorado Class	27
31. USS *West Virginia*, BB-48, Colorado Class	27
32. Japan's *Furutaka*	28
33. USS *New Orleans*, CA-32, New Orleans Class	28
34. Japan's *Amagiri*	29
35. USS *Helm*, DD-388, Bagby Class	29
36. Japan's *I-68*	30
37. Japan's *HA-19*	31
38. USS *Tautog*, SS-199, Tambor Class	31
39. A6M2 Zero Fighter	32
40. P-40 Warhawk	33
41. P-36 Hawk	33
42. F4F3 Wildcat	34
43. B5N2 Kate Torpedo/High-Level Bomber	35
44. D3A Val Dive Bomber	35
45. B-17B Flying Fortress	36
46. B-18 Bolo	36
47. PBY-5 Catalina	37
48. SBD-2 Dauntless Dive Bomber	37
49. TBD-1 Devastator Torpedo/High-Level Bomber	38
50. Rainbow War Plans	40
51. "Crossing the T"	43
52. Main Force	44
53. Southern Operation, Dec-Jan 41	56
54. Fuchida Chart	61
55. Hawaiian Department Critical Sites	72
56. Battery Hawkins, Early 1920s	81
57. Organization of the Hawaiian Coast Artillery Command	83
58. Organization of the Hawaiian Department Mobile Forces	83
59. Organization of the Hawaiian Air Force	84

Page

60. Battery Hasbrouck, Early 1920s	88
61. Interceptor Command	91
62. USS *Ward*	96
63. Radar Track From Opana Radar Site	97
64. Japanese Planes Prepare for Takeoff, 7 December 1941	100
65. First-Wave Plan	101
66. Wheeler AAF Under Attack, 7 December	102
67. Pearl Harbor at 0757, 7 December 1941	104
68. Torpedo Attack on Pearl Harbor	105
69. Battleship Row as Seen From a Japanese High-Level Bomber	109
70. The USS *Arizona* Exploding After Being Hit by a High-Level Bomb	109
71. Battleship Row After the First Wave	110
72. Lieutenant Commander Samuel G. Fuqua	111
73. Second-Wave Plan	114
74. The USS *Cassin* Resting on the USS *Downes* After the Attack	115
75. The USS *Shaw* Explodes on 7 December	115
76. The USS Nevada on Fire and Trying to Head to Sea	116
77. Twenty-One Winches Right the USS *Oklahoma*	121

Stand Maps

Map to Stands 1-3	64
Map to Stands 4-7	65
Map to Stands 8-10	66

Introduction

Surprise, when it happens to a government, is likely to be a complicated, diffuse, bureaucratic thing. It includes neglect of responsibility, but also responsibility so poorly defined or so ambiguously delegated that action gets lost. It includes gaps in intelligence, but also intelligence that, like a string of pearls too precious to wear, is too sensitive to give to those who need it. It includes the alarm that fails to work, but also the alarm that has gone off so often it has been disconnected. It includes the unalert watchman, but also the one who knows he'll be chewed out by his superior if he gets higher authority out of bed. It includes the contingencies that occur to no one, but also those that everyone assumes somebody else is taking care of. It includes straightforward procrastination, but also decisions protracted by internal disagreement. It includes, in addition, the inability of individual human beings to rise to the occasion until they are sure it is the occasion which is usually too late. Finally . . . surprise may include some measure of genuine novelty introduced by the enemy, and possibly some sheer bad luck.*

In his farsighted foreword to Roberta Wohlstetter's excellent book about our failures before Pearl Harbor, Thomas C. Schelling described how and why the Japanese were able to successfully attack the US Pacific Fleet at Pearl Harbor in 1941. Prophetically, his words ring true in describing the successful al-Qaeda attack against the United States on 11 September 2001.

On 7 December 1941 the United States suffered a devastating surprise attack that thrust it into a worldwide war. Our enemy had extensively planned the attack, conducted detailed reconnaissance of its target to determine how to achieve the most destruction, and had innovatively planned the operation to overcome all obstacles. Two services that needed to work together were never ordered to do so, losing synergy that was sorely needed. The United States had indications that an attack was possible but had no single agency to gather all of the available information for an analysis that would suggest an attack. When the attack started, there were indications that something large was happening, but the word was never spread, and our enemy's attack was devastating.

Sixty years later the United States was again thrust it into a worldwide

1

war. On 11 September 2001 enemies of our nation conducted an overwhelming surprise attack against our homeland. Our enemy had again meticulously planned the operation and conducted extensive reconnaissance of its targets before its destructive attacks. Many agencies in our government had indications of an attack, but again, there was no single agency that analyzed all available intelligence to provide us a warning. As word of the attack spread, people refused to accept that the impossible was happening, and again our enemy delivered an overwhelming attack.

As our nation prosecutes the global war on terrorism, it is imperative that we in the profession of arms study those events in which our homeland has been successfully and directly attacked in the past. While attacking our enemies around the world, we must first ensure that our homeland remains completely protected and safe. Not only should we study the tactics, techniques, and procedures of recent operations, but we also need to study history—events where we analyze the actions of both attacked and defender so we are better prepared to handle similar situations that may arise in the future. We should study what mistakes we made and what things we did well as well as the enemy's successes and failures. We must do all of this to increase our ability to prevent another attack on the United States.

The United States is a nation in which it is easy to move about and see, even in a time of war, and our homeland is now a part of the battlespace, a target for our enemies. How do we prevent an enemy from observing a target when it is not overtly breaking the law? Our many intelligence agencies provide outstanding intelligence, but how do we gather all of the information to synergistically determine our enemies' intentions and get this information to the commanders who need it? Our job is to keep America safe, and even when we are in the midst of fighting a war, it is critical that we take the time to study the past so we do not make the same mistakes in the future.

A staff ride has three distinct phases—a preliminary study, a field study, and integration (see *The Staff Ride* by Dr. William G. Robertson, published by the Center of Military History, for information on planning and conducting staff rides). The preliminary study phase prepares students to travel to the field and can be conducted through individual study, instructor-led lectures, discussion, or a combination of these. The field study phase allows students to better understand historical events by studying them from actual locations. Finally, the integration phase allows the students to understand what happened, why it happened, and most important, what can be learned by studying the battle.

The *Staff Ride Handbook for the Attack on Pearl Harbor, 7 December 1941* provides a systematic approach to analyzing how Japan planned for the attack, the failures the United States made in preventing it, and the attack's disastrous results. Throughout the book, pragmatic comparisons of 7 December 1941 and 11 September 2001 are presented for analysis and discussion. Part I describes the organization of the Japanese and American forces, detailing their respective ships, aircraft, strategy, tactics, and logistics. Part II consists of a campaign overview that encompasses the road to war, planning, and intelligence, allowing students to understand how the forces met on the battlefield.

Part III consists of a suggested route to use in conducting a staff ride of the attack on Pearl Harbor. For each stop, or "stand," there is a set of travel directions, an orientation, a description of the action or event that occurred there, and most important, a list of discussion points that a staff ride leader can explore at each stand. Part IV provides information on conducting the integration phase of this staff ride and suggests areas to discuss during the integration phase. Part V provides administrative information on conducting a staff ride at Pearl Harbor, including sources of assistance and logistics considerations. Appendix A provides the Japanese order of battle at Pearl Harbor while Appendix B provides the order of battle of American forces in Hawaii during the battle. Appendix C gives brief biographical information on key participants. Appendix D is a list of Medal of Honor recipients from the Pearl Harbor attack. An annotated bibliography provides sources for preliminary study.

All dates used in this book are Hawaiian time (Japan is one day ahead of Hawaii). The attack on Pearl Harbor occurred on 7 December, which was 8 December in Japan.

---

*Roberta Wohlstetter, *Pearl Harbor: Warning and Decision* (Stanford, CA: Stanford University Press, 1962), viii.

I. The Militaries

US Organization

In 1941 Franklin D. Roosevelt was the President of the United States and, as such, was Commander in Chief of the Army and Navy. He was assisted by the Secretary of War who oversaw the Army, including the Army Air Forces, and the Secretary of the Navy who oversaw the Navy and the Marine Corps.

The Secretary of War in 1941 was Henry L. Stimson, who was 74 years old (see figure 1). Stimson had served as the Secretary of War, 1911-1913; Secretary of State, 1929-1933; and had begun his second term as Secretary of War in July 1940. The Army Chief of Staff was General George C. Marshall, 60 years old at the time of the attack, who had been Chief of Staff since 1939. Under Marshall were three deputy chiefs of staff and his staff (the G1, G2, G3, and G4 and the War Plans Division).

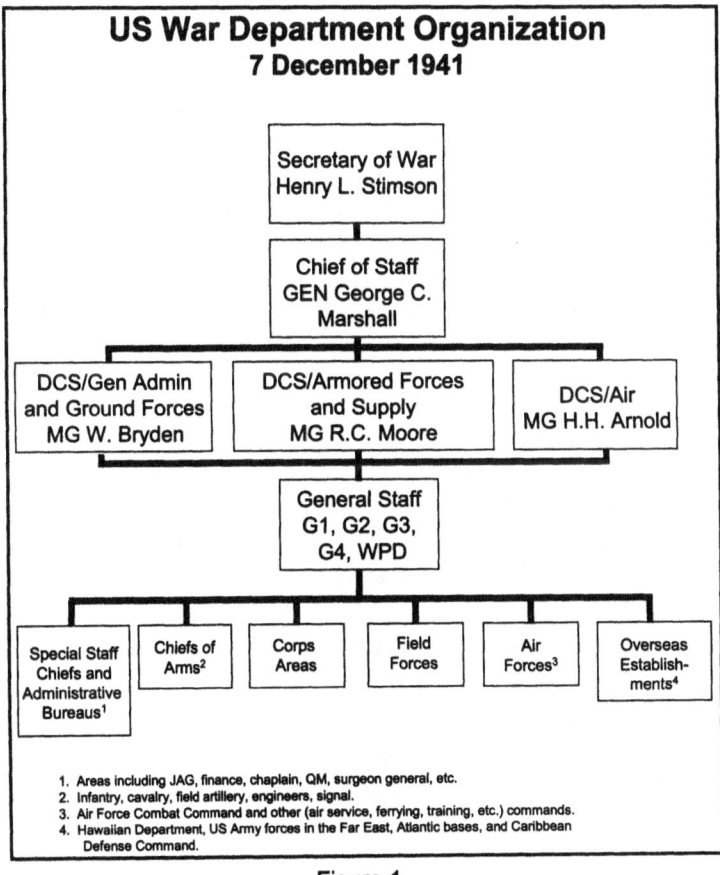

Figure 1.

Under the General Staff were six different component groupings. The first group was the chiefs of the service and administrative bureaus (ordnance, quartermaster [QM], judge advocate general [JAG], finance, etc.) that kept the Army's administration, supply, and services straight. Next were the chiefs of arms, the branches responsible for doctrine and training the soldiers assigned to the field forces. The continental United States (CONUS) was geographically divided into nine corps areas, the headquarters of which were responsible for training, administration of, and mobilizing Regular Army, Reserve, and National Guard units within their corps areas. The Chief of Staff was also the commander of the field forces, the "warfighters" of the Army. Field forces were broken down into a CONUS section and an overseas establishment. Air forces was the fifth component grouping, which was broken down into combat commands (the numbered air forces) and other commands (training, ferrying, etc.).

The last component, which was really a subcomponent of the field forces, was overseas establishments. It was broken down into four subcomponents: the Hawaiian Department, US forces in the Far East, Atlantic bases, and the Caribbean Defense Command. In December 1941 the Army had 1,600,000 men on active duty. The US Army's Hawaiian Department (see figure 2) had 42,857 men in December 1941 and was commanded by Lieutenant General (LTG) Walter C. Short, who was 61. The Hawaiian Department's mission was to defend the Pearl Harbor Naval Base against attack from the air, by expeditionary forces, enemy fleets, or sympathizers. To do this, Short had two understrength divisions, four antiaircraft (AA) regiments, four harbor defense regiments (two incomplete), a bombardment wing, a pursuit wing, aircraft warning units, and other support units.

The Hawaiian Department was plagued by shortages of vital equipment. The air defense regiments had 86 of 98 authorized 3-inch AA guns, 20 of 120 37-millimeter (mm) guns, and 113 of 246 .50-caliber machine guns. The Hawaiian Army Air Force had only 12 of the modern B-17s, 33 B-18s (obsolete), and 12 A-20s. For fighters, it had 99 modern P-40s and 53 obsolete P-36s and P-26s. The Hawaiian Department was also short extended-range reconnaissance aircraft. The aircraft warning units had only received three of six authorized long-range fixed radar sets, but the National Park Service held up installation on property that it controlled, so on 7 December none were operational. The Hawaiian Department additionally had six mobile radar sets, but due to a lack of qualified crews, they were only operational a few hours each day.

The Secretary of the Navy in 1941 was Frank Knox, who was 67. At

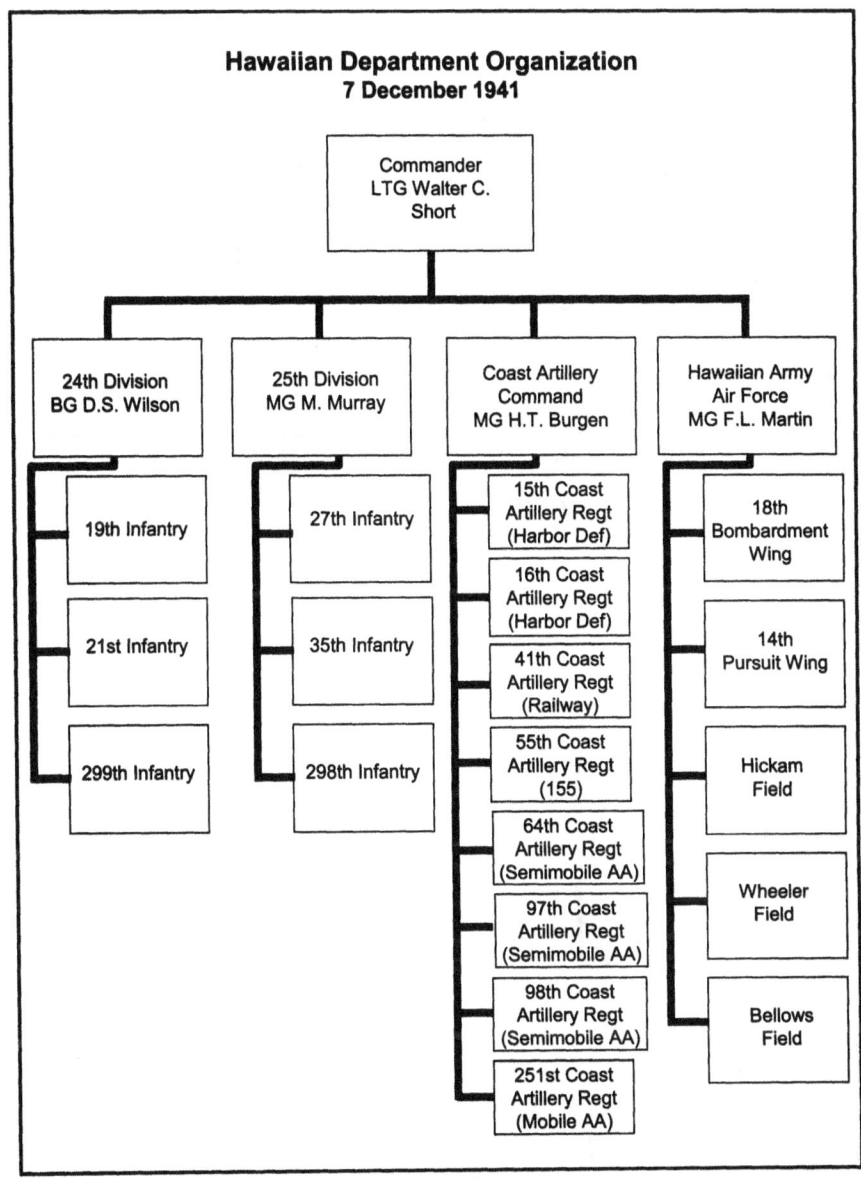

Figure 2.

the outbreak of the Spanish-American War, Knox enlisted and joined Theodore Roosevelt's "Rough Riders." Knox was impressed with Roosevelt and became one of his main advisers. Knox had been a newspaperman. Starting as a reporter, he worked his way up to general manager of all of William Randolph Hearst's newspapers and finally to become the publisher of the Chicago Tribune. Despite being a Republican, Franklin Roosevelt appointed him Secretary of the Navy. Knox's Chief of Naval Operations (CNO) was Admiral Harold R. Stark, who was 61 and had spent his career as a battleship and cruiser man.

The Navy Department's organization (see figure 3) was similar to that of the War Department, but there were some differences. Like the War Department, there were many administrative and logistics bureaus (ordnance, supplies and accounts, and ships), but unlike the War Department, the Navy bureaus worked directly for the Secretary of the Navy. The CNO coordinated with these agencies, but he had no direct command authority. The US Marine Corps (USMC) also directly reported to the Secretary of the Navy.

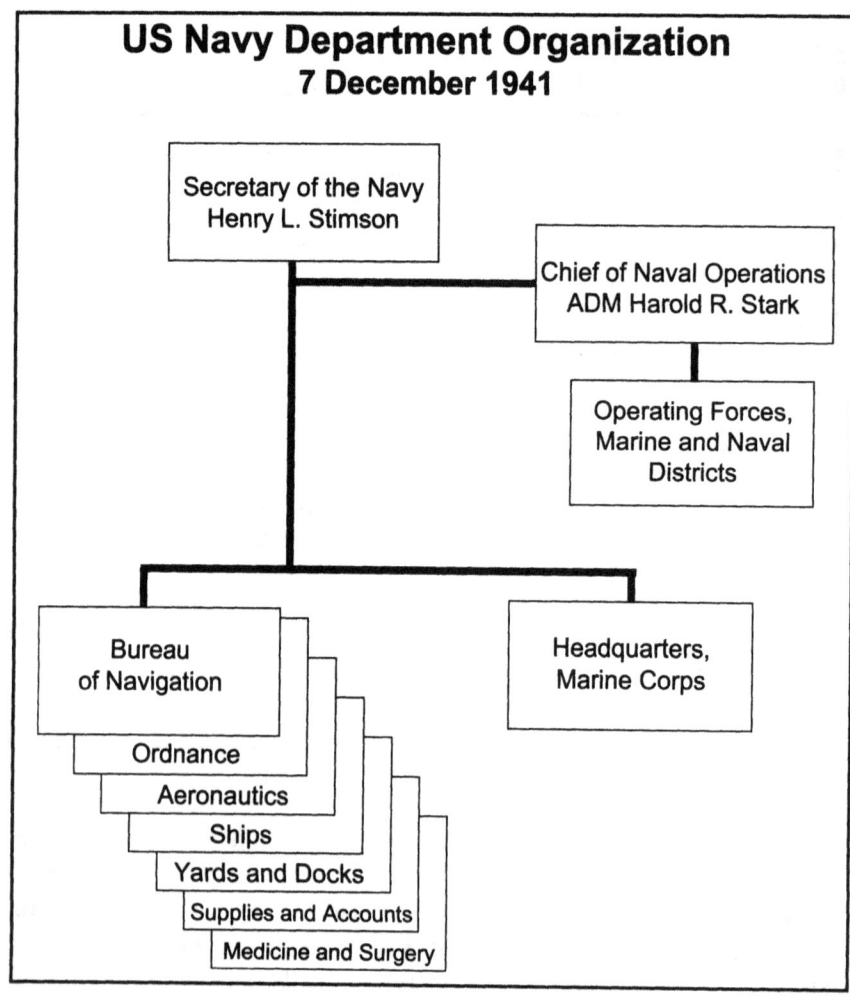

Figure 3.

The CNO was the Navy's warfighter (see figure 4) and was charged with "the operations of the fleet, and with preparation and readiness of plans for its use in war. . . ." The CNO's main warfighting subordinates were the commanders of the Atlantic Fleet, Pacific Fleet, and Asiatic Fleet. The senior of these three fleet commanders was also designated as the Commander, US Fleet, whose mission was to command if two or more fleets were combined. The Naval Coastal Frontier Forces were responsible for defending ports and other coastal areas deemed important to the Navy. The special task forces were groupings of ships task organized and assembled for particular missions, and once the mission was complete they were disbanded. Special duty ships were ships that performed specific missions, such as surveys, that the Navy only had a few of. The Navy Transportation

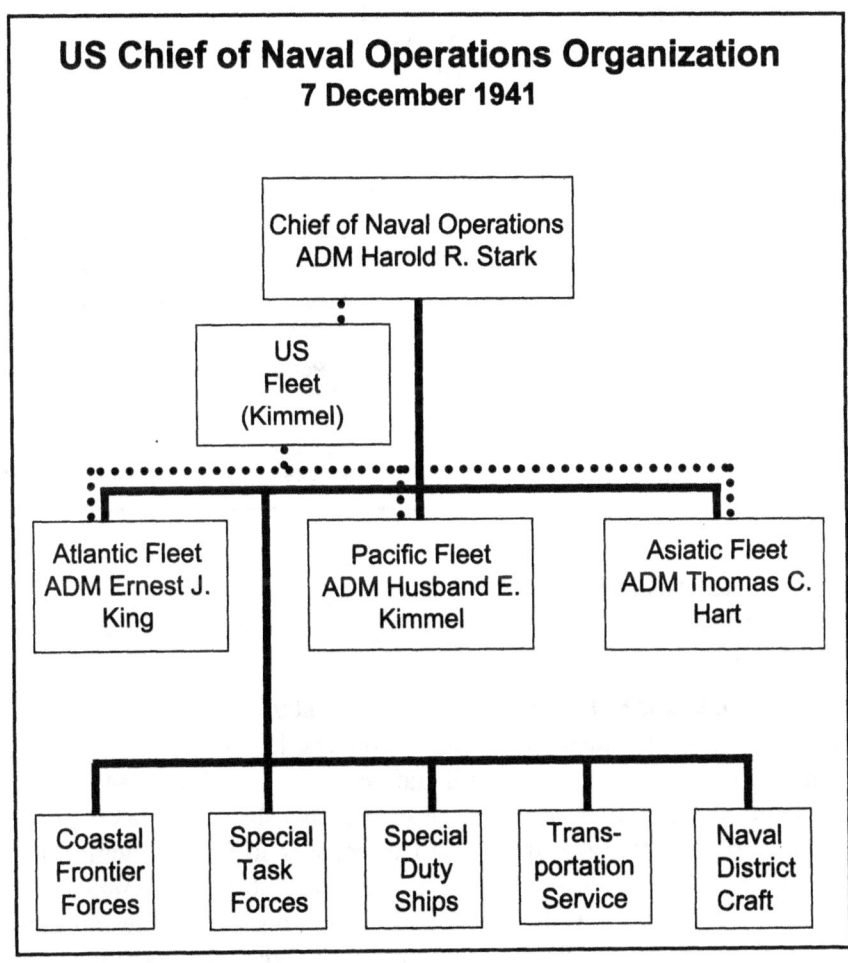

Figure 4.

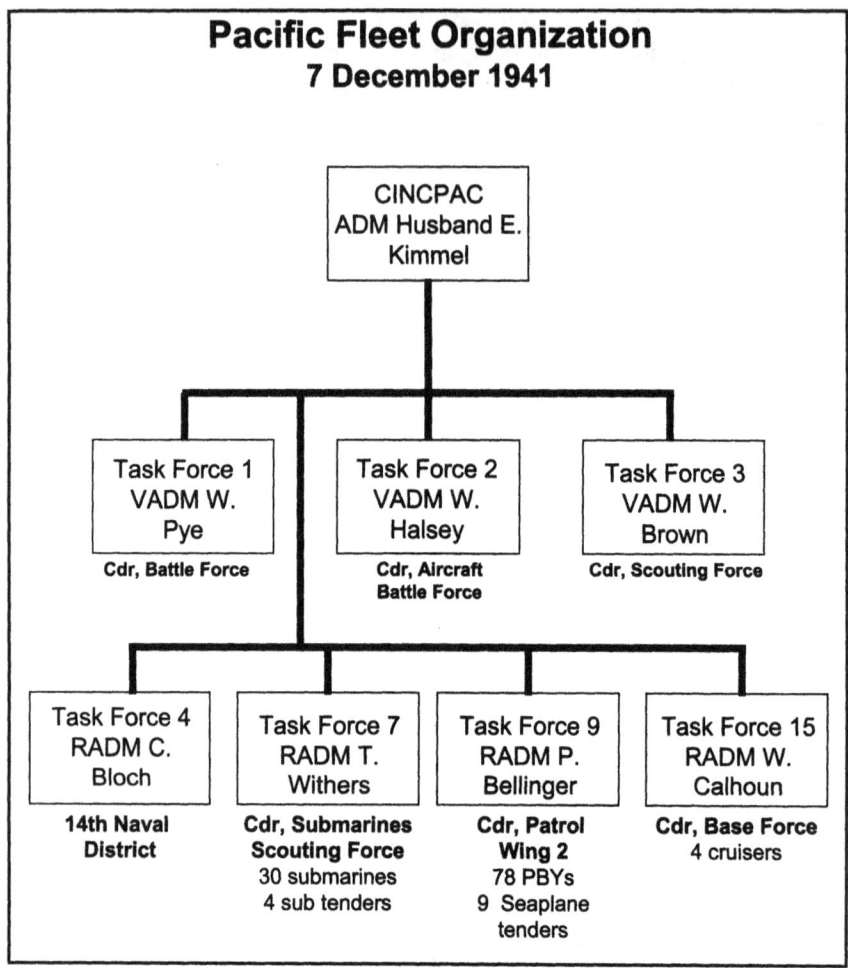

Figure 5.

Service was responsible for all logistics shipping while the naval district craft were specific craft assigned to support naval districts (floating dry docks, submarine chasers, etc.).

On 7 December 1941 the US Navy had 800 commissioned vessels (eight carriers, 17 battleships, 18 heavy cruisers, 19 light cruisers, 171 destroyers, 112 submarines, 87 patrol craft, 66 minecraft ships, 184 tenders, 67 supply ships, 37 transports, and 14 special duty ships) and 284,000 men serving (plus 54,000 marines). The Commander in Chief, Pacific Fleet (CINCPAC) since February 1941 was Admiral Husband E. Kimmel, who was 59 years old. He had spent his career serving as a battleship man. Kimmel organized the Pacific Fleet into task forces for operations and training (see figure 5). Task Forces 1, 2, and 3 were the main warfighting task forces. Task Force 4 was the naval district commanded by Rear Admiral Claude C. Bloch. Its mission was to organize, train, and develop the bases—Pearl Harbor, Midway, and Wake—and provide service to fleet units engaged in operations.

Task Force 7, under the command of Rear Admiral Thomas Withers, was a submarine force whose mission was to provide submarine operations for offensive operations, either independently or in conjunction with other fleet units or bases. Rear Admiral Patrick Bellinger commanded Task Force 9 whose mission was to provide long-range air scouting and air striking forces for the fleet. Task Force 15 was commanded by Rear Admiral William Calhoun and was responsible for protecting trans-Pacific shipping. In December 1941 the Pacific Fleet had three aircraft carriers, nine battleships, 22 cruisers, and 53 destroyers.

Vice Admiral William Pye (see figure 6) commanded Task Force 1,

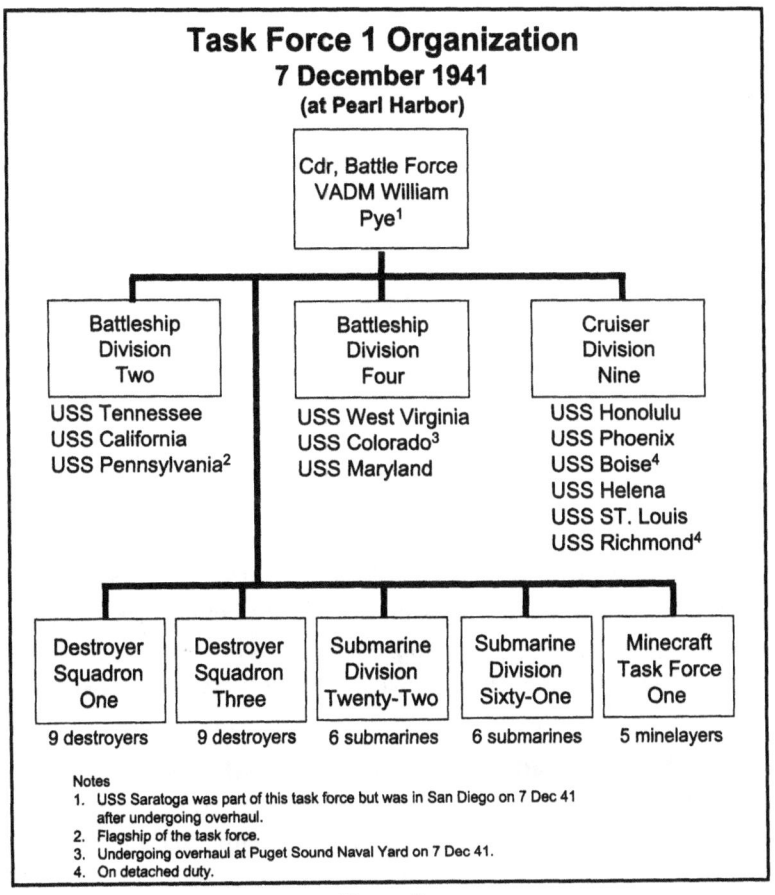

Figure 6.

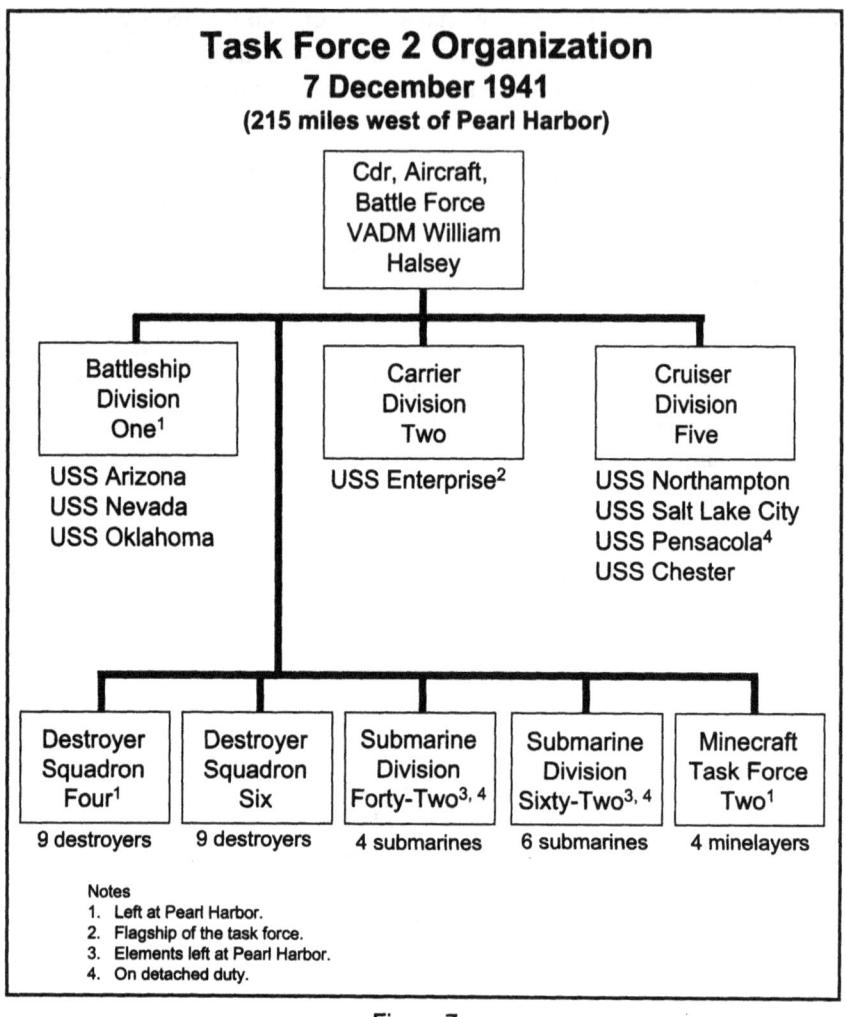

Figure 7.

which had an aircraft carrier, six battleships, and six cruisers. Task Force 1's missions were to cover the operations of any other task force and to engage an enemy in fleet action. In December 1941 Task Force 1's aircraft carrier and one of its battleships were on the west coast of the United States undergoing overhaul.

Vice Admiral William Halsey commanded Task Force 2, which had an aircraft carrier, three battleships, and four cruisers (see figure 7). Its mission was to conduct raids on enemy objectives, particularly on land. On 28 November 1941 Kimmel organized Task Force 8—Task Force 2's carrier, cruisers, and half of its destroyers—and sent it to Wake Island to deliver

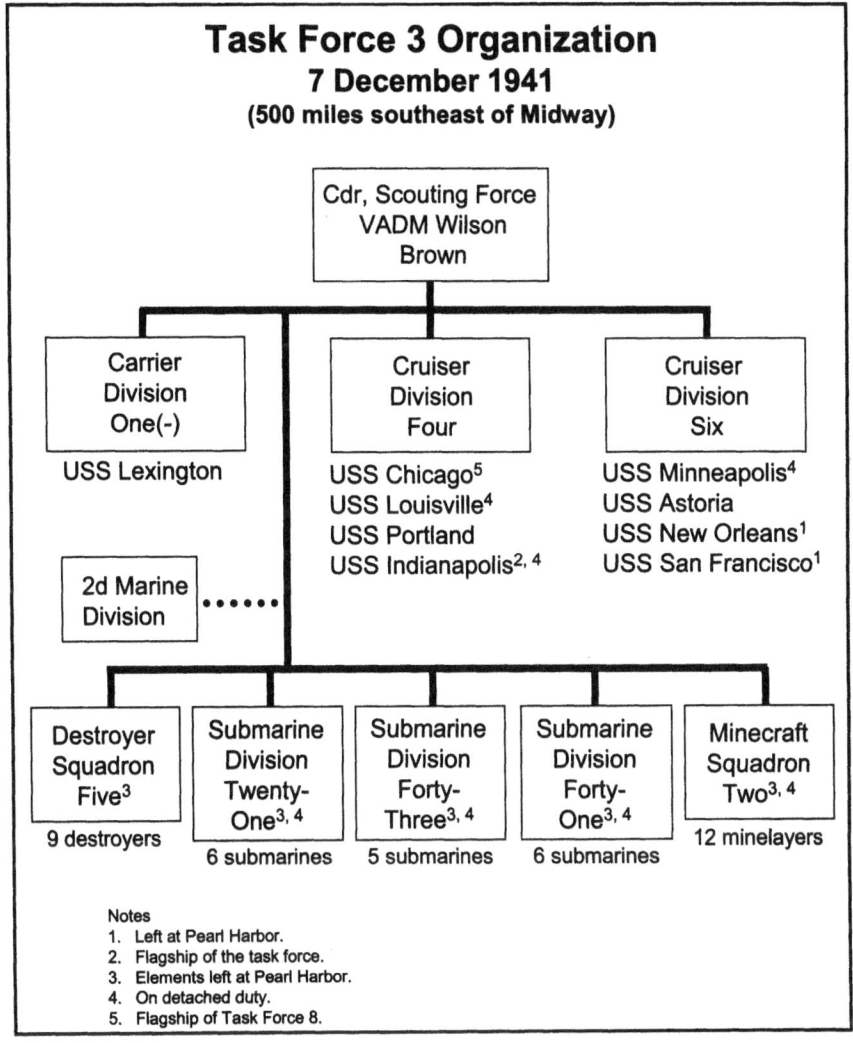

Figure 8.

some marine fighters. It was 250 miles away from Pearl Harbor when the attack began.

Task Force 3 (see figure 8) was commanded by Vice Admiral William Brown and was composed of an aircraft carrier and eight cruisers that could have the 2d Marine Division attached for operations. Its mission was to capture enemy land objectives and to conduct amphibious operations. Kimmel organized Task Force 12 out of Task Force 3 (the carrier, three cruisers, and five destroyers), which on 5 December 1941 left Pearl Harbor to deliver bombers to the marines on Midway. It was 500 miles southeast of Midway when the attack started.

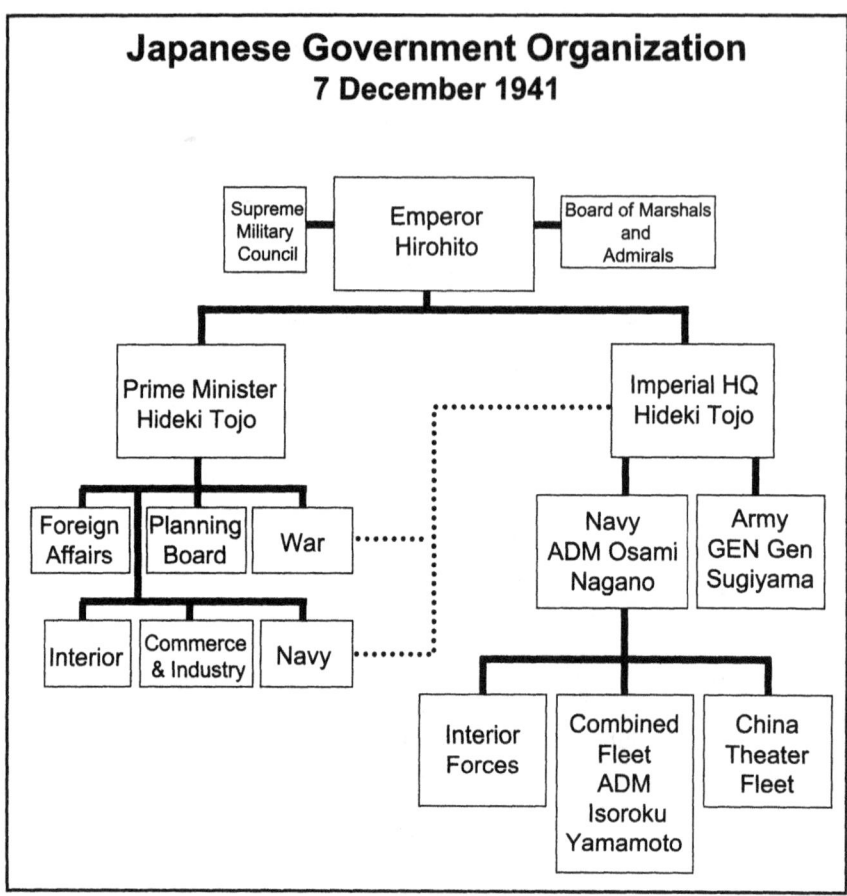

Figure 9.

The USMC had a small component on Oahu. Marine Air Group 21 was at Ewa Field and had Marine Corps Bombing Squadron (VMB)-232, Marine Utility Squadron (VMJ)-252, Fixed-Wing Marine Fighter Squadron (VMF)-211 (Rear Echelon), and VMB-231 (Rear Echelon). Together these squadrons had 10 fighters, 29 bombers, and eight other aircraft. The marines had a ground element at Pearl Harbor consisting of the 1st Defense Battalion(-), 2d Engineer Battalion, 3d Defense Battalion, and 4th Defense Battalion. The marine ground element had 652 men, 12 AA guns, and 36 machine guns. Sixteen ships (eight battleships, two heavy cruisers, four light cruisers, and two auxiliaries) had USMC detachments embarked.

Japanese Organization

Emperor Hirohito of Japan (see figuure 9) was the head of state, not the head of government. The Japanese people considered him half god, half man. He was 41 years old in 1941 and had been emperor for 15 years. The emperor presided over all cabinet meetings (although he did not say a word during the meetings) and had to approve all matters of state, although he always approved items that were presented to him. Military commanders kept him informed on all military subjects. Hirohito had a Supreme Military Council and a Board of Marshals and Admirals, but these were only advisory boards that had no real authority.

Hideki Tojo, who had served in the army and the government for 36 years, was the prime minister and the de facto dictator of Japan. Besides being prime minister, he was also war minister and chief of the Imperial Staff. As prime minister, he had ministers serving underneath him (foreign affairs, interior, etc.) and as war minister and chief of the Imperial Staff, he dominated military affairs. He believed in the theory of total war and believed Japan needed to expand to capture those areas rich in natural resources that Japan lacked. As chief of the Imperial Staff, he had complete command of the Japanese military.

Under the Imperial Staff were the army and the navy. The Chief of the Army General Staff was General Gen Sugiyama who had been minister of war when Japan invaded China, but with Tojo now over him, Sugiyama's powers were limited.

The Chief of the Naval General Staff was Admiral Osami Nagano who was the oldest serving officer in the Japanese navy. He had previously served as vice chief of the General Staff, navy minister, and commander, Combined Fleet. Nagano had three main subordinate elements under him: the Interior Forces that controlled the naval districts and ports; the China Theater Fleet (composed of a few cruisers and destroyers but mainly patrol and gunboats), which was prosecuting the war in China; and the Combined Fleet, the main power of the Japanese navy. In December 1941 the Japanese navy had 10 aircraft carriers, 10 battleships, 38 cruisers, and 110 destroyers.

Admiral Isoroku Yamamoto commanded the Japanese Combined Fleet. Yamamoto had started his career in cruisers (where he lost two fingers at the Battle of Tsushima) and battleships. He later studied at Harvard and had served as the Japanese naval attaché in Washington, DC. While not a pilot himself, Yamamoto became an air power advocate while commanding an air training base and an aircraft carrier division.

In 1941 the Combined Fleet was a mighty armada consisting of 10 subordinate fleets and units (see figure 10). Yamamoto kept three battleships and three cruisers under his direct control. The 1st Fleet was the

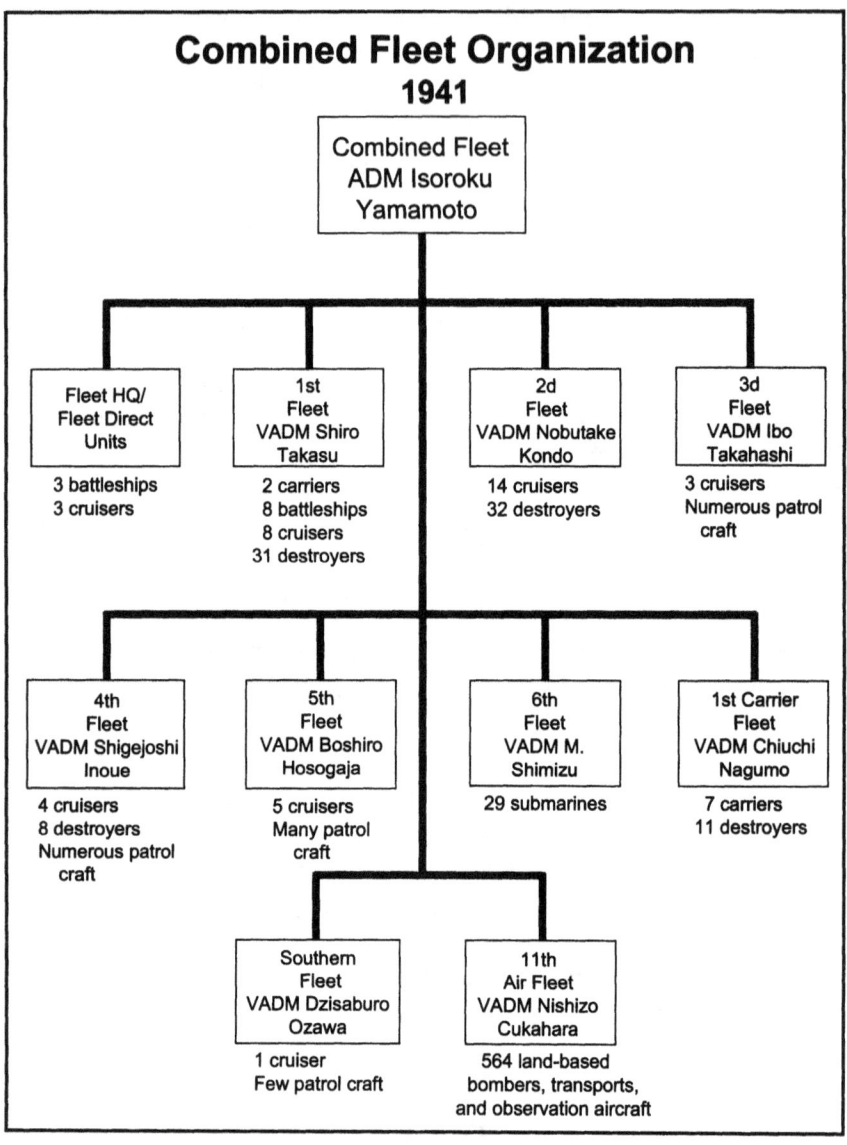

Figure 10.

Battle Force of the Combined Fleet, charged with destroying any enemy fleet. The 2d Fleet was the scouting force, and the 3d Fleet was the blockade and transport force. The 4th and 5th Fleets were charged with defending the Mandated Islands—the Marshalls, Carolines, and Marianas. The 6th Fleet was the submarine force while all of the seaborne aircraft striking power was in the 1st Carrier Fleet. The Southern Fleet was responsible for operations south of and excluding China, and the 11th Air Fleet was the

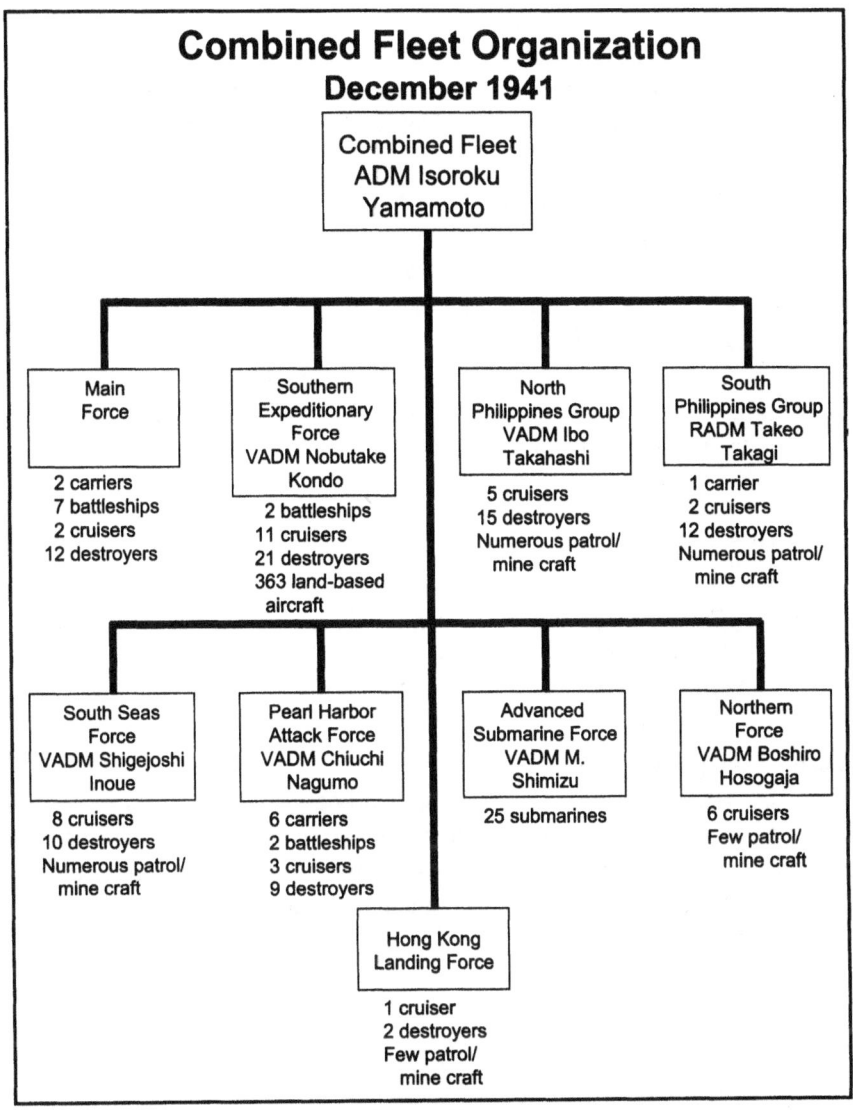

Figure 11.

land-based air-striking force of the Combined Fleet. It had Nell and Betty bombers, flying boat observation aircraft, and transports.

As war with the Western Powers became inevitable, Yamamoto reorganized the Combined Fleet to support the numerous operations it was tasked to conduct (see figure 11). Built around the 2d Fleet, the Southern Expeditionary Force was responsible for operations during the landings in Malaysia. The North Philippines Group was built from the 3d Fleet and was responsible for operations around the northern half of the Philippine invasion. The South Philippines Group was created by taking ships from different fleets and was responsible for operations around the southern half of the Philippine invasion. The 4th Fleet was the nucleus of the South Seas Force; it was to defend the Mandate Islands while also supporting operations during the landings on Guam and Wake Island. The Pearl Harbor Attack Force was built around the 1st Carrier Fleet and was tasked to destroy the US Pacific Fleet while the 6th Fleet became the advanced submarine force that would conduct reconnaissance, downed pilot picket, and attack missions to support the Pearl Harbor operation. The 5th Fleet became the Northern Force that was responsible for defending the northern portion of the Mandate Islands. The Hong Kong Landing Force was fashioned from other fleets and supported the landings at Hong Kong.

Ships

Aircraft Carriers

Navies understood the significance of air power soon after the Wright Brothers took their first flight. In 1908 the US Navy sent observers to watch the Wright Brothers demonstrate their plane to the US Army, and the Navy asked the Wright Brothers to create an aircraft that could be launched from a ship, but they were not interested. The Navy turned to Glenn Curtiss who accepted the project. On 14 November 1910 Eugene B. Ely, an employee of Curtiss, launched his plane from a specially constructed platform on the light cruiser USS *Birmingham*. After this successful test, naval aviation prospered. Curtiss soon invented a plane and ship system whereby a seaplane could land next to a ship, be winched aboard, and be lowered back to the sea to take off again.

Figure 12. HMS *Argus*.

On 19 July 1918 the British conducted the first carrier strike in history. Seven planes took off from the HMS *Furious* and attacked Zeppelin sheds at Tondern, Germany. The planes, however, had to ditch in the ocean because the *Furious'* deck was not set up for landing. The HMS *Argus* was the first true carrier, and it was launched in November 1918.

In 1922 the United States launched its first aircraft carrier, the USS *Langley*, which was a converted collier. The United States added two more carriers, the *Lexington* and *Saratoga*, in the 1920s by converting battle cruisers that were under construction. In 1934 the US Navy commissioned the USS *Ranger*, the first US aircraft carrier built as a carrier from the keel up. By December 1941 the United States had seven fleet carriers and one escort carrier. Three of these carriers were assigned to the Pacific Fleet.

The Japanese also learned to incorporate aircraft carriers into their fleet. Their first carrier was the IJN *Wakamiya*, which was a seaplane tender, but late in its career, it received a platform from which to launch aircraft. Japan also converted battle cruisers into aircraft carriers, and in 1925 it launched the *Akagi*, soon followed by the *Kaga*. By December 1941 the Japanese had 10 fleet carriers.

Japanese Aircraft Carriers

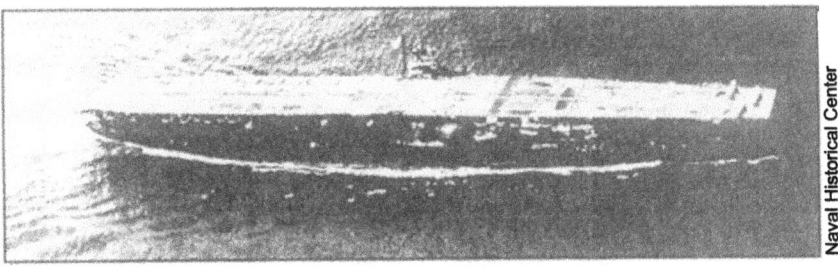

Figure 13. *Akagi*.

Converted from a battle cruiser during construction.
Completed in 1927; overhauled 1935-38.
Displacement: 36,500 tons
Maximum speed: 31 knots
Crew: 2,000
Aircraft: 72 (91 in an emergency)

Figure 14. *Kaga.*
Converted from a battle cruiser during construction.
Completed in 1928; overhauled 1934-35.
Displacement: 38,200 tons
Maximum speed: 28 knots
Crew: 2,016
Aircraft: 72 (90 in an emergency)

Figure 15. *Soryu.*
Converted from a flight deck cruiser during construction.
Completed in 1939.
Displacement: 18,800 tons
Maximum speed: 34 knots
Crew: 1,100
Aircraft: 63 (71 in an emergency)

Figure 16. *Hiryu.*
Converted from a flight deck cruiser during construction.
Completed in 1939.
Displacement: 20,250 tons
Maximum speed: 34 knots
Crew: 1,101
Aircraft: 63 (73 in an emergency)

Figure 17. *Shokaku*.

Completed in August 1941.
Displacement: 36,000 tons
Maximum speed: 34 knots
Crew: 1,660
Aircraft: 72 (84 in an emergency)

Figure 18. *Zuikaku*.

Completed in September 1941.
Displacement: 36,600 tons
Maximum speed: 34 knots
Crew: 1,660
Aircraft: 72 (84 in an emergency)

American Aircraft Carriers

Figure 19. USS *Lexington*, CV-2.

Converted from a battle cruiser during construction.
Completed in 1928.
Displacement: 41,000 tons
Maximum speed: 34 knots
Crew: 2,122
Aircraft: 81

Figure 20. USS *Saratoga*, CV-3.

Converted from a battle cruiser during construction.
Completed in 1928.
Displacement: 33,000 tons
Maximum speed: 34 knots
Crew: 2,111
Aircraft: 81

Figure 21. USS *Enterprise*, CV-6.

Completed in 1938.
Displacement: 19,800 tons
Maximum speed: 33 knots
Crew: 2,919
Aircraft: 90

Battleships

Battleships had been the mainstay of fleets for generations. As early as the 1850s, nations had been designating their main, big gun ships as "battleships." As technology improved, nations kept building larger, better-armored ships, and technology also allowed larger guns to be produced for these heavily armored but slow ships. An example of this era of ships is the USS *Ohio*, which was completed in 1904, displaced 12,000 tons, had a maximum speed of 18 knots, and was armed with four 12-inch guns, 16 6-inch guns, and other smaller weapons.

At the Battle of Tsushima in 1905, the opponents started firing at 19,000 yards, questioning whether the secondary armaments (6-, 8-, and 9-inch guns) were needed on battleships. Because of this phenomenon, the United States and England began work on classes of all "big gun" battleships. The British won the race when they completed the HMS *Dreadnaught* in 1906. It displaced 18,000 tons, had a maximum speed of 21 knots (due to steam turbine engines), and was armed with 10 12-inch guns. Its speed, armor, and firepower made all previous battleships obsolete. Nations scrambled to build all "big gun" battleships so that by 1941 nations were building battleships that displaced 35,000 tons, could reach speeds of 27 knots, and had 16-inch guns.

Japanese Battleships

Figure 22. *Hiei*.

Built as a battle cruiser; converted to a battleship during overhaul.
Completed in 1914; overhauled 1936-40.
Displacement: 29,300 tons
Maximum speed: 27 knots
Crew: 1,221
Armament: eight 14-inch guns, 16 6-inch guns, eight 5-inch AA guns

Figure 23. *Kirishima*.

Built as a battle cruiser; converted to a battleship during overhaul.
Completed in 1915; overhauled 1927-30, 1935-36.
Displacement: 32,000 tons
Maximum speed: 28 knots
Crew: 1,200
Armament: eight 14-inch guns, 16 6-inch guns, eight 5-inch AA guns

American Battleships

Figure 24. USS *Nevada*, BB-36, Nevada class.

Completed in 1916; overhauled 1927-30.
Displacement: 27,500 tons
Maximum speed: 20 knots
Crew: 1,552
Armament: 10 14-inch guns, 24 5-inch guns

Figure 25. USS *Oklahoma*, BB-37, Nevada class.

Completed in 1916; overhauled 1927-29.
Displacement: 27,500 tons
Maximum speed: 21 knots
Crew: 1,552
Armament: 10 14-inch guns, 24 5-inch guns

Figure 26. USS *Pennsylvania*, BB-38, Pennsylvania class.

Completed in 1916; overhauled 1940-41.
Displacement: 31,400 tons
Maximum speed: 21 knots
Crew: 1,620
Armament: 12 14-inch guns, 24 5-inch guns

Figure 27. USS *Arizona*, BB-39, Pennsylvania class.

Completed in 1916; overhauled 1929-31.
Displacement: 31,400 tons
Maximum speed: 21 knots
Crew: 1,588
Armament: 12 14-inch guns, 24 5-inch guns

Figure 28. USS *Tennessee*, BB-43, Tennessee class.

Completed in 1920.
Displacement: 33,100 tons
Maximum speed: 21 knots
Crew: 1,625
Armament: 12 14-inch guns, 16 5-inch guns

Figure 29. USS *California*, BB-44, Tennessee class.

Completed in 1921; overhauled 1929-30.
Displacement: 32,300 tons
Maximum speed: 21 knots
Crew: 1,623
Armament: 12 14-inch guns, 16 5-inch guns

Figure 30. USS *Maryland*, BB-46, Colorado class.

Completed in 1921.
Displacement: 32,600 tons
Maximum speed: 21 knots
Crew: 1,623
Armament: eight 16-inch guns, 18 5-inch guns

Figure 31. USS *West Virginia*, BB-48, Colorado class.

Completed in 1923.
Displacement: 33,590 tons
Maximum speed: 21 knots
Crew: 1,626
Armament: eight 16-inch guns, 26 5-inch guns

Cruisers

Cruisers were lightly armored, heavily armed, fast ships designed to screen formations and to scout out enemy fleets. Their survivability depended on speed, not armor. Japan developed classes of battle cruisers armed with 14-inch guns, but they were converted to battleships during overhauling. The United States and Japan had each decided to build a new class of battle cruiser (lightly armored but armed with 14- or 16-inch guns), but the limitations of the Washington Naval Treaty of 1922 only allowed cruisers to displace 10,000 tons or less so cruisers became smaller and more lightly armed. By 1941 Japan had 38 cruisers, and the US Pacific Fleet had 21 cruisers. Each side had different classes, and a sample of a cruiser from each side follows.

Figure 32. Japan's *Furutaka*.

Completed in 1926.
Displacement: 10,507 tons
Maximum speed: 33 knots
Crew: 625
Armament: six 8-inch guns, four 4.7-inch guns,
  eight 24-inch torpedo tubes, 42 25mm guns

Figure 33. USS *New Orleans*, CA-32, New Orleans class.

Completed in 1923.
Displacement: 9,950 tons
Maximum speed: 33 knots
Crew: 708
Armament: nine 8-inch guns,
  eight 5-inch guns, 16 40mm guns

Destroyers

Destroyers had been around since the 1890s. Originally named "Torpedo Boat Destroyers," these ships were small, fast, and armed with rapid-firing guns to destroy enemy torpedo boats. With the invention of the submarine, destroyers took on the antisubmarine mission, and the name of this type of ship was shortened to "destroyer." By 1941 navies used destroyers as screening vessels, scouting vessels, anti-torpedo-boat ships, and antisubmarine ships. By 1941 Japan had 110 destroyers, and the US Pacific Fleet had 53. Each side had different classes, and a sample of a destroyer from each side follows.

Figure 34. Japan's *Amagiri*.

Completed in 1928.
Displacement: 2,090 tons
Maximum speed: 38 knots
Crew: 197
Armament: six 5-inch guns,
 18 depth charges, nine 24-inch torpedo tubes

Figure 35. USS *Helm*, DD-388, Bagley class.

Completed in 1928.
Displacement: 1,850 tons
Maximum speed: 36.5 knots
Crew: 158
Armament: four 5-inch guns, 12 21-inch torpedo tubes

Submarines

Navies had experimented with submarines since the 1860s, and as technology increased, the submarine's capabilities improved greatly. During World War I, Germany sank more than 5,000 Allied ships using their submarines, but these era submarines were limited by range, so postwar improvements led to submarines that could cross the Atlantic or Pacific Oceans easily and return.

The United States started seriously working to acquire a submarine fleet in the late 1890s, and in 1900 it launched its first submarine. From 1900-41 the United States continued to improve its submarine fleet.

In 1905 Japan was locked in combat with Russia and looked for asymmetric ways to defeat the superior Russian navy and started acquiring submarines. Their first five submarines were purchased from the United States. After the war with Russia, Japan developed its own submarines and continued to improve them, developing numerous types including seaplane carriers, mine warfare submarines, and midget submarines. By 1941 Japan had 65 fleet submarines, and the US Pacific Fleet had 23. Each side had different classes, and a sample of a submarine from each side follows.

Figure 36. Japan's *I-68*.

Completed in 1934.
Displacement: 1.400 tons
Maximum speed: 23 knots surface, 8 knots submerged
Crew: 84
Armament: six 53-centimeter (cm)
   torpedo tubes, one 10cm gun

Figure 37. Japan's *HA-19*.

Completed in 1938.
Displacement: 46 tons
Maximum speed: 23 knots surface,
  19 knots submerged
Crew: 2
Armament: two 53cm torpedo tubes

Figure 38. USS *Tautog*, SS-199, Tambor class.

Completed in 1934.
Displacement: 1.475 tons
Maximum speed: 20 knots surface, 9 knots submerged
Crew: 65
Armament: 10 21-inch torpedo tubes, one 3-inch gun

Aircraft

Fighters

Military use of aircraft predates the invention of the airplane. As early as the 1860s, nations used balloons to conduct reconnaissance of enemy positions. Militaries first employed aircraft in observation roles to gain valuable information on the enemy, and during World War I nations started arming their aircraft so they could destroy any enemy observation aircraft that appeared. These early armed aircraft were termed "fighting scouts." They were plagued with very short range and, as such, were defensive aircraft. As aviation technology improved during the war, nations were able to increase their fighters' range, and they were used to attack ground targets. Air superiority became a prerequisite for any operation; militaries wanted control of the air so they could prevent the enemy from using their aircraft to attack and observe while they used their own to attack the enemy. Allied air superiority over the Central Powers was an important aspect of their victory in World War I.

After World War I technological advances improved the fighter's performance as metal replaced wood in aircraft structure and aerodynamics improved to allow the monoplane to replace the biplane. Other improvements included adding optical sights, more and bigger machine guns, radio communications, and retractable landing gear. By 1941 fighters were both an effective offensive and defensive weapon. In the offensive role, fighters protected other aircraft, and if there were no enemy fighters, they could be employed to strafe targets. In the defensive role, fighters could remain at their base, and once a threat was detected, take off and attack the enemy.

Japanese Fighter

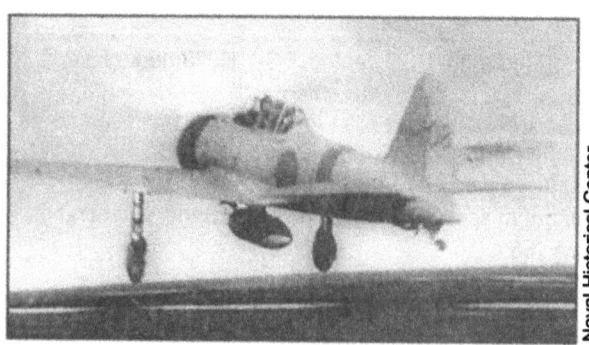

Figure 39. A6M2 Zero fighter.

User: Army and Navy
Crew: 1
Speed: 340 miles per hour (mph)
Range: 1,160 miles
Armament: two 20mm cannons, two 7.7mm machine guns

American Fighters

Figure 40. P-40 Warhawk.

User: Army
Crew: 1
Speed: 362 mph
Range: 850 miles, 1,200 with auxiliary tank
Armament: six .50-caliber machine guns,
  up to 700 pounds (lb) of bombs

Figure 41. P-36 Hawk.

User: Army
Crew: 1
Speed: 313 mph
Range: 830 miles
Armament: two .30- or .50-caliber machine guns

Figure 42. F4F3 Wildcat.

User: Navy and Marine Corps
Crew: 1
Speed: 320 mph
Range: 770 miles
Armament: six .50-caliber machine guns, 200 lb of bombs

Bombers

As aircraft took on the role of attack, pilots soon carried small bombs with them to drop on the enemy. Nations saw the utility of being able to deliver bombs from the air and developed aircraft whose primary mission was to drop bombs. Dirigibles were employed to deliver bombs, but soon technological advances allowed the construction of larger aircraft that could deliver bigger payloads. During World War I, large bombers were used to attack enemy homelands. The Germans used the Gotha bomber to bomb London while the British used the Handley-Page bomber to bomb Germany. After the war, technology allowed for bigger and better bombers as aerodynamics and engine improvements led to larger bombers with bigger payloads and the ability to carry machine guns for self-protection and optical sighting improvements led to increased bombing accuracy.

Tests during the interwar period led many innovators to believe that air power could attack and destroy ships, a fact not lost on farsighted naval officers. Navies developed bombers that could be launched from ships, and while smaller than land-based bombers, seaborne bombers could deliver devastating strikes against ships. Navies also developed dive bombers—airplanes designed to carry smaller bombs that started their attack high above the target, then dove on their target in a steep dive, thus increasing accuracy. Torpedoes had devastating effects against shipping in World War I, so navies developed airplanes that could skim across the water and deliver torpedoes against enemy ships. Some navies also used these torpedo planes as high-level bombers because they were able to carry heavy loads.

Japanese Bombers

Figure 43. B5N2 Kate torpedo/high-level bomber.

User: Navy
Crew: 3
Speed: 235 mph
Range: 683 miles
Armament: two 7.7mm machine guns in cowling,
  one 7.77mm machine gun in rear cockpit,
  one 1,750-lb torpedo or 1,750 lb of bombs

Figure 44. D3A Val dive bomber.

User: Navy
Crew: 2
Speed: 281 mph
Range: 874 miles
Armament: two 7.7mm machine guns over the engine,
  one 7.7mm machine gun in rear cockpit, one 550-lb bomb

American Bombers

Figure 45. B-17B Flying Fortress.

User: Army
Crew: 6
Speed: 292 mph
Range: 3,000 miles
Armament: seven .50-caliber machine guns, 6,000 lb of bombs

Figure 46. B-18 Bolo.

User: Army
Crew: 6
Speed: 217 mph
Range: 1,200 miles
Armament: three .30-caliber machine guns,
 4,400 lb of bombs

Figure 47. PBY-5 Catalina.

User: Navy
Crew: 7 to 9
Speed: 189 mph
Range: 2,900 miles
Armament: two .50-caliber machine guns,
  4,000 lb of bombs/depth charges/torpedo

Figure 48. SBD-2 Dauntless dive bomber.

User: Navy and Marine Corps
Crew: 2
Speed: 255 mph
Range: 1,345 miles
Armament: two .50-caliber machine guns forward,
  two .30-caliber machine guns in rear cockpit,
  1,600 lb of bombs

Figure 49. TBD-1 Devastator torpedo/high-level bomber.

User: Navy
Crew: 2 to 3
Speed: 207 mph
Range: 700 miles
Armament: one .50-caliber machine gun forward,
   one .30-caliber machine gun in rear cockpit,
   1960 lb of bombs/torpedoes

Strategy

Despite the fact that Japan had been an ally during World War I, American war planning in the interwar years focused on war with Japan, and Japanese planning focused on the United States. Responsibility for US joint strategic war plans fell to the Joint Board, which had been organized in 1903. From its inception through World War I, the Joint Board was ineffectual and produced little of strategic value, so it was reorganized in 1919 to provide some real jointness to war planning. The Board now consisted of six members—the Army Chief of Staff, Chief of Naval Operations (CNO), their deputies, and their chiefs of war plans. Additionally, the Joint Planning Committee was formed to give the Joint Board a staff for joint war planning, and the Army and Navy each provided four officers from its War Plans Division to conduct the detailed preparations of joint plans. The Joint Planning Committee started work on a series of war plans that focused on fighting one enemy at a time. The plans were named "color plans" because each potential enemy was a different color—orange for Japan, red for England, etc. The plans the Joint Planning Committee produced were the basis for developing subordinate supporting plans for each of the services.

The original series of Orange Plans for war against Japan called for offensive naval war against Japan. To accomplish this, the Navy needed a base in the Far East to service the entire US Fleet, and Manila provided the only capable port west of Pearl Harbor. Therefore, the Army's responsibility became to defend and hold Manila Bay until the US Fleet arrived with Army reinforcements.

Diplomatic actions hindered US planning for war with Japan during the 1920s and 1930s. In 1922 the United States signed the Five Power Naval Treaty that called for the United States, Japan, Great Britain, France, and Italy to not fortify any of their Far Eastern possessions. Japan never had plans to fortify any of its positions in the Mandate Islands, and this treaty ensured that the Philippines, Guam, and Hong Kong could not become fortresses in Japan's backyard.

Politicians and diplomats, in response to the devastation of World War I, looked for ways to prevent war, and treaties and agreements seemed like the answer. The Washington Naval Conference of 1922 led to an agreement whereby the United States, Great Britain, and Japan would limit their capital ships based on the ratio 5-to-5-to-3. On paper, this seemed like a bargain for the United States and Britain because their navies could be 40-percent larger than Japan's. The problem was that the United States and Britain had to reduce their navies (the United States scrapped 15 battleships and cruisers that had been under construction) while the Japanese had to build up to get to their "limitation." With the stroke of a pen, Japan reduced the size of the US Navy while being allowed to increase the size of its own navy.

While writing joint war plans was important to US war planners, by 1937 they realized that their basic assumption of having to fight only one enemy at a time was doubtful. In 1936 and 1937 Japan, Germany, and Italy had executed a number of agreements that created what became known as the Axis Alliance. The possibility of having to simultaneously fight in the Atlantic and Pacific forced planners to reassess their assumptions. The Joint Board and the Joint Planning Committee focused on the problem, and in 1939 they developed guidelines for a new series of war plans called the "Rainbow" plans. This name signified that multiple potential enemies were involved, thus different color plans were combined. The planners developed five Rainbow war plans, numbered one through five, all of which first provided for the defense of the Western Hemisphere in accordance with the Monroe Doctrine (see figure 50).

Rainbow 1 assumed the United States would fight without allies and would focus action in the Atlantic while maintaining a strategic defensive

Rainbow War Plans

Plan	Allies	Primary Area	Secondary Area
1	None	Atlantic	Pacific
2	Britain, France	Pacific	Atlantic (limited)
3	None	Pacific	Atlantic
4	None	South Atlantic	Pacific
5	Britain, France	Atlantic	Pacific

Figure 50. Rainbow war plans.

in the Pacific. When the situation in the Atlantic allowed, the United States would concentrate in the Pacific. Rainbow 2 assumed that the United States would fight with Britain and France and, therefore, could focus on the Pacific. Rainbow 3 assumed that the United States would fight without allies and would concentrate on the Pacific first. Rainbow 4 was similar to Rainbow 1—the United States would not have any allies and would have to focus on the Atlantic—but this plan called for the Army to be sent to South America for operations. Rainbow 5 specified that the United States would be allied with Britain and France, and would ensure the defeat of Germany before concentrating on Japan.

With the start of World War II and after the fall of France, the US planners reconsidered all of their alternatives. Western Europe had fallen, Britain was barely hanging on, and if it fell, Germany and Japan could attack the Western Hemisphere. Reinforcing England seemed to be the logical priority in any war situation. CNO Admiral Harold Stark produced what has been called Plan Dog (because the recommendation was contained in paragraph D, "Dog," in the phonetic alphabet of the time). Stark's analysis indicated that it was key to the United States to ensure Britain did not fall. If it did, Germany and Italy would likely expand into the Western Hemisphere, and retaining England, as a staging base for future land actions against the European continent, was imperative. Stark thought that Britain did not have the manpower and was too weak economically to fight alone so he recommended that the United States assist Britain in any way possible. His recommendations were accepted, and the Atlantic became the primary theater of operations.

Japan had desired to be the most powerful nation in the Far East since the 1890s. As part of that plan, Japan had to expand to acquire areas that were rich in natural resources not available in Japan and to form a protective outer ring away from the home islands. With victories over the Russians and Chinese in the late 1890s/early 1900s, Japan had obtained Formosa, Korea, the Kuril Islands, and parts of Manchuria. As an ally at the end of World War I, Japan was mandated from Germany possession of the Marshall Islands, the Caroline Islands, and the Mariana Islands. Japan thought the best way to be the foremost power of the Far East was through economics, so the United States, the real economic competitor in the area, became the most likely adversary.

Despite diplomatic successes (the Five-Power Naval Limitation Treaty, Washington Naval Conference, etc.), Japan was still militarily inferior to the United States and had to develop a plan for war that ensured victory. Because of the limitations of the Washington naval treaty, the Japanese looked for ways to gain any naval advantage. Its submarine fleet was wanting (and there were no treaty limitations on submarines), so Japan concentrated on improving and increasing it. Additionally, the treaty limited the tonnage of cruisers and battleships but allowed ships under construction to be converted to aircraft carriers of limited tonnage (of which the Japanese underreported the size of its new carriers). With improved submarine and aircraft carrier capabilities, but with an inferior capital ship ratio, Japan developed the concept of "Kantai Kessen" (decisive fleet battle).

Kantai Kessen assumed that any war with the United States would be primarily a naval war. Therefore, Japan wanted the fight to be near the Japanese home islands. They envisioned the United States sailing a large fleet toward Japan. Along the way Japanese submarines would track and attrit the US fleet. The Americans would have to bypass Japanese bases on the Mandate Islands, which could then be used to attack the fleet from the air and would also be astride the lengthening US line of communication. As the now-attrited US fleet approached the Japanese home islands, the main Japanese fleet, supported by land-based air power, would fight and defeat the US fleet.

Operational

In response to the Rainbow plans, the US Pacific Fleet reorganized (see figure 5). Rainbow 5 was the most likely plan to be executed, so in July 1941 Kimmel issued his own plan for executing Rainbow 5. Since the United States' main effort was the Atlantic, Kimmel developed a plan that defended Hawaii and the West Coast while simultaneously setting the conditions for future operations. At the outbreak of war, the Pacific Fleet would sweep the ocean of all Japanese shipping west of Hawaii, conduct reconnaissance and raids on the Marshall Islands, move the 2d Marine Division to Hawaii, and prepare to invade the Marshall Islands. Once these tasks were completed, the Pacific Fleet would seize Truk Island in the Marshall Islands to use as an advanced fleet base in subsequent operations. Eventually, the Pacific Fleet would seize all of the Marshall and the Caroline Islands. Once the Pacific Fleet had seized the Marshall and Caroline Islands, it would develop plans for subsequent operations. Other tasks assigned to the Pacific Fleet were defending Guam, protecting the sea lines of communication, and defending territory in the Pacific to prevent Japanese expansion into the Western Hemisphere. The purpose of these operations was to divert enemy strength away from the western Pacific to "support the forces of the associated powers in the Far East."

The Japanese developed plans for executing Kantai Kessen, and the Combined Fleet was organized to execute the plan (see figure 10). The 6th Fleet of the Combined Fleet had three types of submarines to support Kantai Kessen. Scouting submarines equipped with seaplanes would locate and maintain contact with the US fleet. Command submarines would coordinate raids by attack submarines and cruisers from the 2d Fleet. As the US fleet steamed west, it would be attacked from the air by land-based bombers from the 11th Air Fleet stationed in the Mandate Islands. The 1st Carrier Fleet's aircraft would locate the American carriers and attack them with dive bombers to destroy their flight decks, attempting to prevent American air operations. As the US fleet neared the home islands, more submarines would lay minefields and launch midget submarines to continue to attrit the enemy. Once within range of Japan, more land-based aircraft of the 11th Air Fleet would attack the US fleet. The 1st Fleet's battleships and heavy cruisers would clear away any US screening forces so that swift light cruisers and destroyers could sweep in for massed torpedo attacks. At this point, the battleships and heavy cruisers would join the fight to finish off the American fleet.

Tactics

Naval tactics of the 1940s were based on time-tested principles of getting as much steel on a target as fast as possible. Fleets had a submarine component whose mission was to locate and track enemy fleets, with the secondary mission of attacking smaller combat vessels or logistics ships. Scouting forces were a major part of any fleet, and their purpose in the offense was to locate and attack the enemy fleet with high-speed cruisers and destroyers using torpedoes. Additionally, the scouting forces' speed allowed them to get ahead of an enemy's main force to "cross the T" (the process of steaming in line across the front of an enemy line, thus allowing you to maximize fire on the enemy while he cannot bring all of his guns to bear on you. (See figure 51.)

In the defense, the scouting force would protect the main fleet by preventing the enemy's scouting force from locating and/or attacking the main fleet and attacking the enemy main fleet as it closed. Aircraft carriers were used to launch aircraft to locate enemy fleets and to control the gunfire of the battleships and cruisers. Eventually, dive bombers were developed to strike an enemy carrier's flight deck so it could not launch its own aircraft. Torpedo planes could be used in conjunction with torpedo attacks by cruisers and destroyers. The battle force of any fleet was the main fighting unit of any navy. Large battleships and battle cruisers, supported by faster light cruisers and destroyers, would maneuver to gain position on the enemy. The preferred tactic was to cross the T, but doctrine ex-

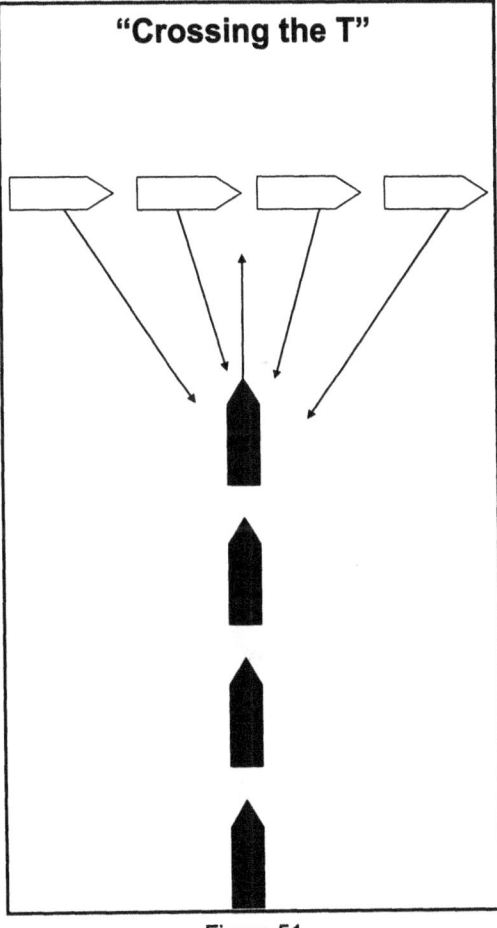

Figure 51.

isted for parallel attacks, either steaming in the same direction or sailing opposite the enemy (see figure 52). The keys to success for any naval engagement were maneuvering to gain an advantageous position on your enemy and the crews' gunnery skills; those who could hit targets from great distances would win the battle.

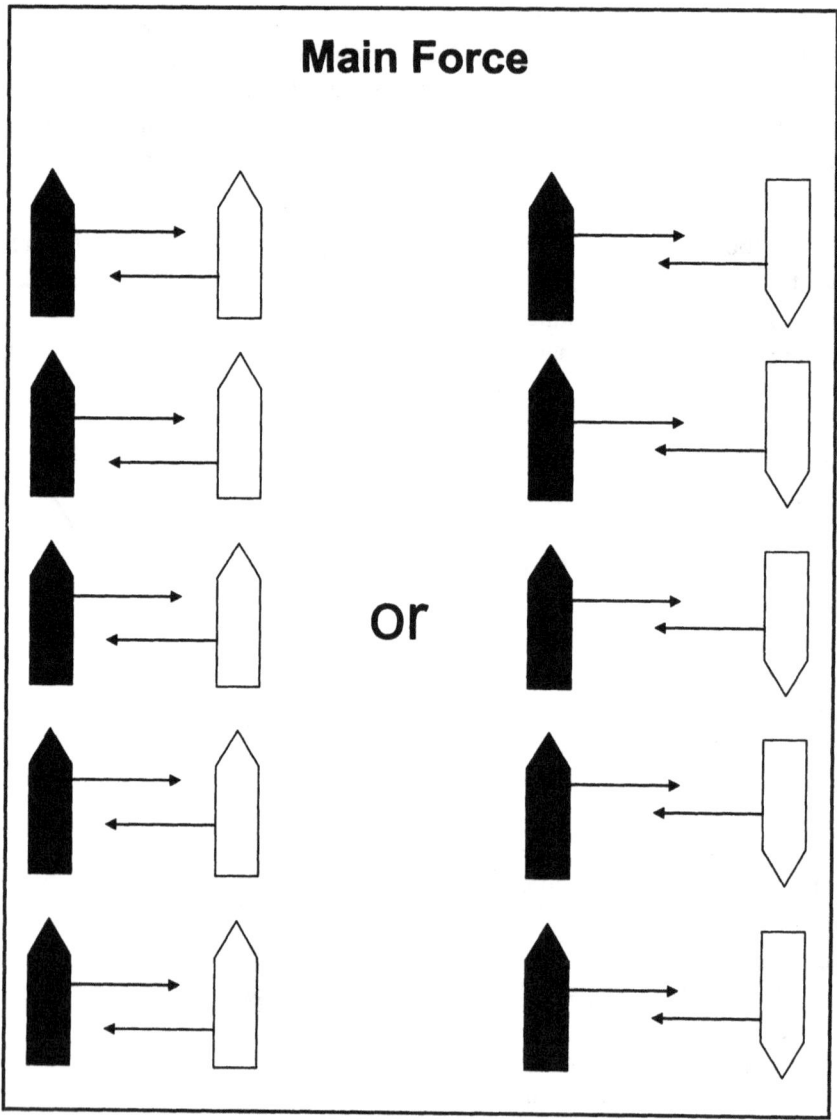

Figure 52.

Logistics

Due to the distances involved in the Pacific, logistics was a concern to both sides. The US fleet had its main ports and naval yards along theUS West Coast at Puget Sound and San Diego. These yards could resupply, refit, repair, and completely overhaul ships. In 1940 Pearl Harbor was the home base of the Hawaiian Detachment (a carrier, a cruiser, and some destroyers), but it possessed only limited capabilities. Ships could refit, refuel, and rearm, but major repairs and overhauls still had to be accomplished on the West Coast. All across the Pacific, the United States maintained small naval bases at such places as Johnston Island, Midway, Palmyra, American Samoa, Wake Island, and Guam. Each of these small bases maintained an airfield, and some served as submarine bases and/or refuel and rearm points. The Navy Base at Subic Bay in the Philippines was another of the Navy's major bases, but it also only possessed limited capability to refuel, rearm, and repair ships of the fleet.

In 1940 the Pacific Fleet shifted its home port from the West Coast to Pearl Harbor. Immediately, work was started to convert Pearl Harbor into a base that would be capable of supporting the Pacific Fleet with all services required except major repair and overhaul. New docks, dry docks, and fuel tanks were added to the facility, and by 1941 Pearl Harbor was a major base.

The major limitation of ships of the 1930s and 1940s was the amount of fuel they could carry. The ships could carry enough food and water for the sailors, but they needed to stop to refuel. Destroyers had the shortest range and could travel about 6,000 nautical miles at 15 knots before refueling, while battleships could range 13,000 miles and carriers 15,000 miles. Due to the limited ranges, the Navy had to have bases all across the Pacific to service its fleet. In 1941 ships were able to refuel at sea, but it was not a common practice so the Navy still depended on bases to refuel their ships.

Everything the Pacific Fleet (and the smaller Asiatic Fleet in the Philippines) used had to be moved by ship from CONUS to the servicing bases. As part of its organization, the Pacific Fleet had Task Force 4, which was responsible for organizing, training, and developing the bases (Pearl Harbor, Midway, Wake) and providing service to those fleet units engaged in operations. Additionally, Task Force 15 was to secure shipping coming from the United States.

The Navy had limited shipping assets to support its fleet. In 1941 the Navy had the following logistics ships (numbers in parentheses are ships supporting the Pacific Fleet):

Oilers	29	(11)
Munitions ships	4	(2)
Cargo ships	22	(5)
General stores ships	3	(2)
Provisions ships	9	(4)
Transports	37	(8)
Hospital ships	2	(1)

Due to the distances involved, logistics was critical to Japan. Japan maintained its ports and navy yards throughout the home islands. They maintained larger bases at locations, including Yokosuka, Kure, Sasebo, Maizuru, and Bako. These bases could provide all required services for ships up to and including overhaul. There were many smaller yards and bases throughout the home islands that provided more limited support. Japan, like the United States, depended on forward bases for their ships. Their base on Truk Island was the most advanced, with services including refuel, rearming, and repairing. Other bases away from the home islands were Saigon and Formosa. Like the United States, Japan's ships could also refuel while under way, but it was not a practiced skill and was very rarely used.

The Japanese navy had built a lot of ships, but it, like the United States, did not have enough logistics ships to properly support its fleets. In 1941 the Japanese navy had the following logistics ships (numbers in parentheses are ships supporting the Combined Fleet):

Oilers	37	(31)
Munitions ships	1	(1)
Cargo ships	7	(1)
General stores ships	11	(3)
Provisions ships	12	(12)
Transports	64	(59)
Hospital ships	5	(4)

II. Pearl Harbor Campaign Overview

In July 1853 Commodore Matthew Perry, in command of four US Navy ships, arrived at Edo (now Tokyo) under orders from President Millard Fillmore to make contact with the Japanese to open commercial relations with the reclusive nation. The Japan of 1853 was much like the Japan of 1653, a feudal nation of many different clans headed by the warrior class samurai, with a shogun (meaning "general") leader with dictatorial powers. The emperor was the head of state (but not of the government) and Japan's religious leader, but he had no real power. Starting in 1653 the shoguns had kept Japan in isolation; missionaries who attempted to enter the country were killed, traders were driven off, and shipwrecked seamen were imprisoned.

When Perry entered the bay at Edo, the Japanese leaders observed his ships belching smoke and bristling with modern cannons, and while impressed with the show of force, the Japanese would not agree to Perry's terms. He departed, determined to return to complete the mission.

In February 1854 Perry did return, but this time he brought seven warships and a large contingent of marines. Perry came ashore with a marine band leading and immediately started negotiating a treaty with the Japanese. The shogun was intimidated by the power of the United States and reluctantly agreed to the Treaty of Kanagawa, which was signed on 31 March 1858. The treaty called for friendship between the nations, opening two ports for the United States to use, safety guarantees for shipwrecked seamen, and allowances for the United States to acquire supplies and provisions from the Japanese. Soon, other nations arrived to negotiate treaties with Japan, and the once isolationist country was now thrown open to the West.

However, some of the clans in western Japan were upset with the shogun's inability to keep Japan isolated, which led to internal strife for control of the country. What were initially small clashes between the shogun's forces and the western clans led to full-scale war in 1868. For seven months the western clans battled the shogun's supporters, but on 4 July 1868 the western clans won the Battle of Veno and control of the nation. They immediately restored the emperor to power and effectively ended the feudal era.

The new government realized that Japan, now open to the West, had to modernize to achieve equality and immediately implemented measures to attain this goal. Feudalism and its associated samurai class were abolished, modern administrative zones within the country were established, an Imperial Army was raised through conscription, and an Imperial Navy was created by purchasing British ships. To support these efforts, the government organized a banking system that allowed commerce to flourish, created a national school program that preached loyalty to the emperor, and significantly improved the nation's infrastructure. By 1890 Japan was a regional power in the Far East.

In need of raw materials and new markets, Japan fought China in the Sino-Japanese War in 1894-95. Fought in Korea and Manchuria, the Imperial Army and Imperial Navy won numerous victories, forcing China to sue for peace, in which China ceded Korea and Formosa and paid a large indemnity. Russia now intimidated the defeated Chinese and was able to acquire Port Arthur and the Chinese Eastern Railway, which sowed the seeds for future conflict with the Japanese.

Starting in 1900 Japan prepared for war with Russia to ensure it dominated the area and to extract revenge for Russian meddling after the Sino-Japanese War. On 8 February 1904, before war was declared, Japan attacked the Russian Far East fleet in Port Arthur with torpedo boats, causing extensive damage. The now superior Japanese fleet trapped the weakened Russian fleet in the port. Japanese ground troops laid siege to Port Arthur on 25 May 1904 and finally forced the Russian garrison and fleet to surrender on 2 January 1905. Meanwhile, the Russians had decided to move their Baltic fleet to the Far East and after a horrific journey, the numerically superior, but qualitatively inferior, Russian Fleet was destroyed at the Battle of Tsushima on 27 May 1905. Admiral Heihachiro Togo, the fleet commander, became a national hero, and a young ensign named Isoroku Yamamoto, who was serving on one of the Japanese cruisers, was wounded, losing two fingers in the fight. The United States brokered a peace treaty whereby Russia gave up its interests in the area, including Port Arthur. Japan was now the clear power in the Far East.

Japan joined the Allies during World War I, a prudent act for which Japan reaped great rewards. The other allied nations required materials, and Japanese industry flourished as it worked to meet the allied war demands. Japan occupied the German possessions of the Mariana, Caroline, and Marshall Islands, which were mandated to Japan after the war. While only suffering 300 military deaths, Japan expanded its empire to the Central Pacific and also became an industrial power.

After the carnage of World War I, nations were seeking ways to avoid future slaughter, and treaties were completed to accomplish this. Between 1921 and 1934 various nations signed seven major disarmament treaties, but the Washington Naval Conference, 1921-22, had the greatest impact on Japan and the United States as they moved toward World War II. The major points of the resulting treaty were a capital ship tonnage ratio of 5-to-5-to-3 for the United States, Great Britain, and Japan; a 10-year moratorium on capital ship construction; and a prohibition on constructing and improving fortifications of Pacific possessions. On paper this treaty looked like a huge triumph for the United States, but Japan was the true victor.

The treaty allowed the United States to have 525,000 tons of capital ships while Japan could only have 315,000 tons. However, the United States had to decommission ships and stop constructing new ships (15 battleships and battle cruisers) to stay within the limits. As a result, the newest US battleship at Pearl Harbor during the attack was commissioned in 1923. Japan, on the other hand, had to build new ships to get to its limit and also had no plans to reinforce its bases in the Mandated Islands. Concurrently, the treaty prevented Britain and the United States from building fortresses in Japan's "backyard." Ultimately, the only type of ship that all three nations possessed fewer of than the treaty allowed was aircraft carriers. By 1937 both the United States and Japan were working hard to build new aircraft carriers.

In the late 1920s and early 1930s, Japan suffered from the international economic depression. The depression decimated Japan's economy, and the resulting unemployment bolstered the Japanese military's desire to seize parts of China to acquire much-needed natural resources. In September 1931 Japan initiated a war against China. Asserting that China had planned to blow up a Japanese railroad, Japan attacked Chinese troops in Manchuria. By February 1932 Japan had seized Manchuria, renamed it Manchukuo, installed a "puppet" government, and turned it into a Japanese colony. When the League of Nations protested, Japan simply withdrew from the league, which was one of the first steps in the league's ultimate demise.

Japan's desire to expand its empire led to the "China incident," a clash with Chinese troops near the Marco Polo Bridge on 7 July 1937. For the next six months, Japanese troops attacked to the west and south against ineffective Chinese resistance and were able to capture large expanses of territory. Logistics problems and Chinese guerrilla warfare caused the advance to slow but not before Japan had control of a vast amount of territory, including the capitol, Nanking. During the Japanese assault on Nanking, the USS *Panay*, a gunboat, was attacked by Japanese dive bombers and sunk. The attack outraged Americans, and the situation was only settled by a formal Japanese apology and payment of reparations.

Throughout 1938 Japan continued its assault on China by consolidating gains, fighting guerrillas in newly captured areas, and continuing to drive west. In October the Japanese seized the port town of Canton, which gave them control of all of China's main ports. Japan spent 1939 attempting to cut off all supply to the Chinese by capturing all of its remaining ports and concentrating on controlling the areas it occupied. Only the strong will of the Chinese people prevented China's total collapse.

In June 1940 Japan demanded of the French Vichy government permission to land forces in French Indochina. Unable to confront Japan anyway, the Vichy government accepted the demand. The United States, in turn, warned Japan to stay out of French Indochina, but in September Japanese troops started landing and occupying northern parts of French Indochina, quickly occupying and using the airfields and ports. President Franklin D. Roosevelt's administration reacted by placing an embargo on steel and scrap iron from the United States, an event the Japanese termed an "unfriendly act."

The United States wanted Japanese expansion to stop and took severe actions to show its intentions. Congress passed a bill that called for increasing the size of the Navy by 300 percent by 1944. The US Pacific Fleet, home ported in San Diego, was on maneuvers in the Hawaiian Islands in May 1940, and at the end of the maneuvers, President Roosevelt ordered the fleet to remain at Pearl Harbor as a deterrent to the Japanese. Pacific Fleet Commander Admiral James O. Richardson protested against the move because he was concerned about Pearl Harbor's ability to support the fleet logistically. Richardson protested so vehemently that he was relieved and replaced by Admiral Husband E. Kimmel in February 1941.

Kimmel was concerned about not having enough ships to fight the Japanese if a war came, and instead of gaining ships, he lost 25 percent of his fleet. The president and secretary of the Navy decided that the Atlantic Fleet needed to be reinforced because they considered the endeavor to keep the sea line of communication to England open as the main effort. The Atlantic Fleet had to take up part of the escort duty, and to do so, it needed to be reinforced. Kimmel, who had requested reinforcement, instead was ordered to send the aircraft carrier *Yorktown*; the battleships *Mississippi*, *Idaho*, and *New Mexico*; four light cruisers; 17 destroyers; and 16 supply and auxiliary ships to the Atlantic.

On 27 September 1940 Japan allied itself with Germany and Italy by signing the Tripartite Treaty in Berlin where each side promised to aid the others for 10 years, but the treaty did not require Japan to declare war on Britain (who was at war with Germany and Italy).

In July 1941 Japan demanded more Indochinese bases and territory from the Vichy government, and when Japan moved to occupy these bases, the United States and its allies reacted swiftly and harshly. The United States, Great Britain, and the Netherlands froze Japanese assets, but more consequential to the Japanese, they imposed an all-out embargo against Japan, including the export of oil. Japan imported all of the oil it used and had now lost access to almost all of its sources. War in the Pacific grew closer.

Admiral Isoroku Yamamoto assumed duties as commander in chief of Japan's Combined Fleet in August 1939. Yamamoto was not a pilot himself, but he had learned to appreciate the value of naval aviation and had held important naval aviation commands, including duty at the Navy flight school, chief of naval aviation, and command of an aircraft carrier division. Additionally, he held other key assignments, including an extended period of study at Harvard University followed by attaché duty at the US Embassy, duty as a representative at the London Naval Conference, and a tour as the vice minister of the navy. Yamamoto desperately wanted to avoid a war with the United States, but he also wanted to be prepared if war became inevitable or if he was ordered to wage war. Yamamoto's experience taught him the United States' industrial and technological advantage would make a prolonged war between the nations a losing struggle for Japan. He therefore determined that Japan would have to cripple the United States early in the fight so Japanese expansion could prosper to such a degree that the United States would have to sue for peace. He determined that Japan had to have free reign in the Pacific for six months to achieve a chance at victory. He also thought that naval aviation was the tool to crippling the Americans by destroying the US Pacific Fleet. His plan would become known as Operation *HAWAII*.

As early as March 1940, Yamamoto first considered an aerial strike on the US Pacific Fleet, and his thoughts quickly concentrated on Pearl Harbor when the Pacific Fleet moved there in May. Yamamoto first publicly declared his plan in January 1941 when he sent a letter to Navy Minister Admiral Koshiro Oikawa stating that war with the United States had become inevitable and that Japan should "attack and destroy the U.S. main fleet at the outset of the war" and that the attack should be at Pearl Harbor.

Yamamoto did not wait for permission from the Navy Ministry but began gathering the best aviation and naval minds he could to plan the attack. He asked Rear Admiral Takijiro Onishi, Chief of Staff, 11th Air Fleet and a trusted friend, to study the idea. Onishi knew he needed an experienced pilot and planner who was smart, innovative, and fearless so he sent for Commander Minoru Genda, then serving as an air staff officer on the aircraft carrier *Kaga*. Genda was known throughout the Japanese navy as an exceptional aviator and planner, but his writings and arguments about employing air power were radical and alienated him from the "mainline" navy. That made Genda the perfect planner that Onishi needed. Onishi briefed Genda on Yamamoto's concept and asked him to study the feasibility and to draft a report. Genda studied the concept for 10 days and determined the plan was feasible, given nine conditions:

1. The attack had to be a complete surprise.
2. The main objective should be the US aircraft carriers.
3. US land-based aircraft had to be destroyed to gain air superiority.
4. Every available Japanese aircraft carrier should participate.
5. All types of aircraft (torpedo, dive, high-level, fighter) should be used.
6. Fighters had to play an active role.
7. The attack had to be a daylight attack.
8. Japanese ships had to refuel at sea.
9. Attack planning had to be done in strict secrecy.

Yamamoto took Genda's proposal, presented it to his staff, and started it working on gathering information on numerous subjects such as logistics, weather, method of attack, etc. Yamamoto still did not have permission to conduct this planning, but he thought if war came, an attack on Pearl Harbor was the only hope for Japan to have a chance for victory.

Genda's idea of combining the carriers into one organization had been debated throughout the navy for a few years. Opponents of the concept were afraid the concentrated carriers, if located by the enemy, would make an easy target. Proponents believed concentrated carriers allowed for concentrating aircraft for strikes on the enemy, and having the carriers together allowed escorts to mass their abilities to protect the carriers from all enemies—air, surface, and submarine. Yamamoto was in favor of creating the First Air Fleet, and in the end he won out. On 10 April 1941 the Japanese navy created the First Air Fleet by combining the First Carrier Division (two carriers), the Second Carrier Division (two carriers), and the Fourth Carrier Division (one carrier). Now Japan had a command that ensured Yamamoto could easily concentrate the power of his air arm for operations. The pieces of Genda's plan were beginning to fall into place.

Japan had taken the radical step of creating an aircraft carrier fleet but soon blundered when it named Vice Admiral Chuichi Nagumo to command it. The revolutionary carrier fleet needed an innovative thinker and commander, but Nagumo was a conservative, traditional naval officer. He had spent an accomplished career as a surface officer commanding cruisers, battleships, and surface ship divisions, but he had never even served in an aviation assignment. It was now his mission to lead the fleet that would start the war and hopefully set the conditions for victory for Japan.

Nagumo needed a competent staff to help him run his carrier fleet, so most of the exceptional staff officers from the carrier divisions were selected to serve Nagumo. Rear Admiral Ryunosuke Kusaka, an officer with experience commanding two aircraft carriers, was selected as the chief of staff. Perhaps the most important selection was Genda, who joined the First Air Fleet staff as air officer.

Once the First Air Fleet was a reality, training became the priority. The fleet's ships maneuvered as they learned to work together as a fleet, while the aircraft on the carriers trained to conduct attacks against all kinds of targets under all kinds of conditions. The fleet staff worked to solve the problems determined in Genda's nine-point concept. To use all types of aircraft for the attack, fleet staff officers had to determine a technique to use to incorporate the torpedo bombers (military thought of the day deemed Pearl Harbor too shallow for torpedo bombers), and they had to develop a bomb for the high-level bombers that would penetrate a battleship's thick upper deck. Genda was the point man for each of these concerns.

Pearl Harbor was a very shallow port (approximately 40 feet), and Japanese torpedoes, using the current doctrine and equipment, would plunge to the bottom and get mired in the mud. Conventional wisdom said that the problem was insurmountable, but Genda believed the problem could be overcome. He gathered all of the best torpedo plane pilots from the fleet and told them they had to figure out how to employ or modify aerial torpedoes so they did not descend below 33 feet of water. Genda did not tell the pilots why, just that they had to solve the problem. The torpedo plane pilots worked frantically and tried all kinds of ideas before they came up with an acceptable solution. Japanese torpedo planes would fly at 30 to 60 feet altitude (normal attack altitude was 300 feet) at a very slow speed. Additionally, the torpedoes were modified with a large wooden fin on the tail that would break off when the torpedo hit the water but not before reducing the depth of the torpedo's plunge. Once the problem was resolved, Genda assigned the four best "Kate" squadrons to torpedo duty because he believed this would be the most difficult type of attack. The selected crews began an intensive training regimen using the new techniques, still not knowing why.

The high-level bombers caused more of a problem for Genda than the torpedo bombers. Battleships had a thickly armored deck, and numerous large projectiles were needed to destroy a battleship. The Japanese did not have a bomb that could accomplish this. Additionally, the flyers' bombing accuracy was very poor. Many planners would have given up, but Genda was a determined man. He once again assembled the best high-level pilots, and they worked together to solve the dilemma. They made many attempts, and after numerous failures solved the problem by converting 16-inch battleship shells into bombs weighing 800 kilograms (1,700 lb). They discovered that if the bombs were dropped from 11,000 feet, they would penetrate a battleship's deck. To solve the accuracy problem, the high-level bomber leaders implemented three initiatives to improve accuracy. First, they changed from a nine-ship triangle formation to a five-ship triangle formation. Second, every plane in the five-plane group would drop its bomb when the lead plane dropped its. Finally, the best bombardiers were teamed with the best high-level pilots. These hand-picked crews were selected to lead each five-ship formation. The crews also started an intense training routine, which combined with the three initiatives, drastically improved the high-level bombers' accuracy.

The Japanese continued to incorporate Genda's nine points into the plan, but all would be for naught if the First Air Fleet could not figure out how to refuel the ships at sea. For security, the First Air Fleet would travel a little-used northern route to Hawaii, which would preclude any possibility of refueling at a naval base. The older Japanese carriers had very limited ranges because of the belief that they would fight near Japanese home waters, and some of the smaller ships had small fuel tanks that limited their range. To make the attack, the Japanese would have to master the art of refueling at sea. Genda solved this problem using the technique he used solving other problems—he gathered the best tanker ship captains and told them to solve the problem.

The captains realized that the techniques in place (the tanker traveled in front of the ship to be refueled, floated a hose back to it, and refueled the ship) were sound for smaller ships (destroyers and cruisers), but lack of training was the stumbling block. Battleships and aircraft carriers were too big and not maneuverable enough to do this, so the tanker captains learned to follow the big ships and pass the hoses forward. The tankers first rehearsed the procedures with their own ships until they were proficient; then they began training with the First Air Fleet ships. Three refueling exercises were conducted in November, and all of the ships rehearsed refueling as the fleet concentrated before departing for Hawaii. Another obstacle that Genda identified had been overcome by innovative thinkers and training.

Throughout summer 1941 the First Air Fleet continued a vigorous training program with aircrews flying numerous missions at Ariake Bay on Kyushu, the southern most of Japan's four main islands, which remarkably resembled Pearl Harbor. The ships continued maneuvering together, learning to sail and operate as a fleet while the tankers rehearsed their critical operations. The staff continued to refine the plan based on updated intelligence (covered in detail at the first stand) and changing circumstances.

In August Japanese war planning increased as the military leaders realized that war with the United States was more likely everyday. In response to the American embargo, the Imperial Staff developed the "Southern Operation," a plan for capturing the industrial rich Dutch East Indies and Malaya. Japan realized this action would force the United States and Great Britain into war, so the plan also called for seizing the American-held Philippines and Guam and the British possessions of Hong Kong and Burma. Once the southern areas were secured, Japan would occupy strategic positions in the Pacific and fortify them, thus forming a tough defensive perimeter around Japan and its newly acquired resource areas. Once the perimeter was secure, Japan would try to negotiate for peace. The planners thought it would take six months to accomplish all the tasks and had to be free of interference from the American Navy during that time. Yamamoto had the plan for ensuring that the US Pacific Fleet would not interfere for six months.

On 6 August 1941 Yamamoto decided the time was right to brief the naval general staff on the Pearl Harbor attack plan. The naval general staff was considering moving the annual naval exercises from late November to September, and Yamamoto thought the exercise would be a great opportunity to rehearse the Pearl Harbor attack with exercise umpires, which would allow for a general after-action review of the plan. The naval general staff was unenthusiastic about the plan, considering it a gamble with the possible loss of most of Japan's aircraft carriers as a real possibility. Despite its concerns, the staff accepted Yamamoto's plan for further review.

At the end of August and the beginning of September, events occurred that would have enormous benefits for the Pearl Harbor plan. On 24 August Commander Mitsuo Fuchida was assigned to the First Air Fleet as

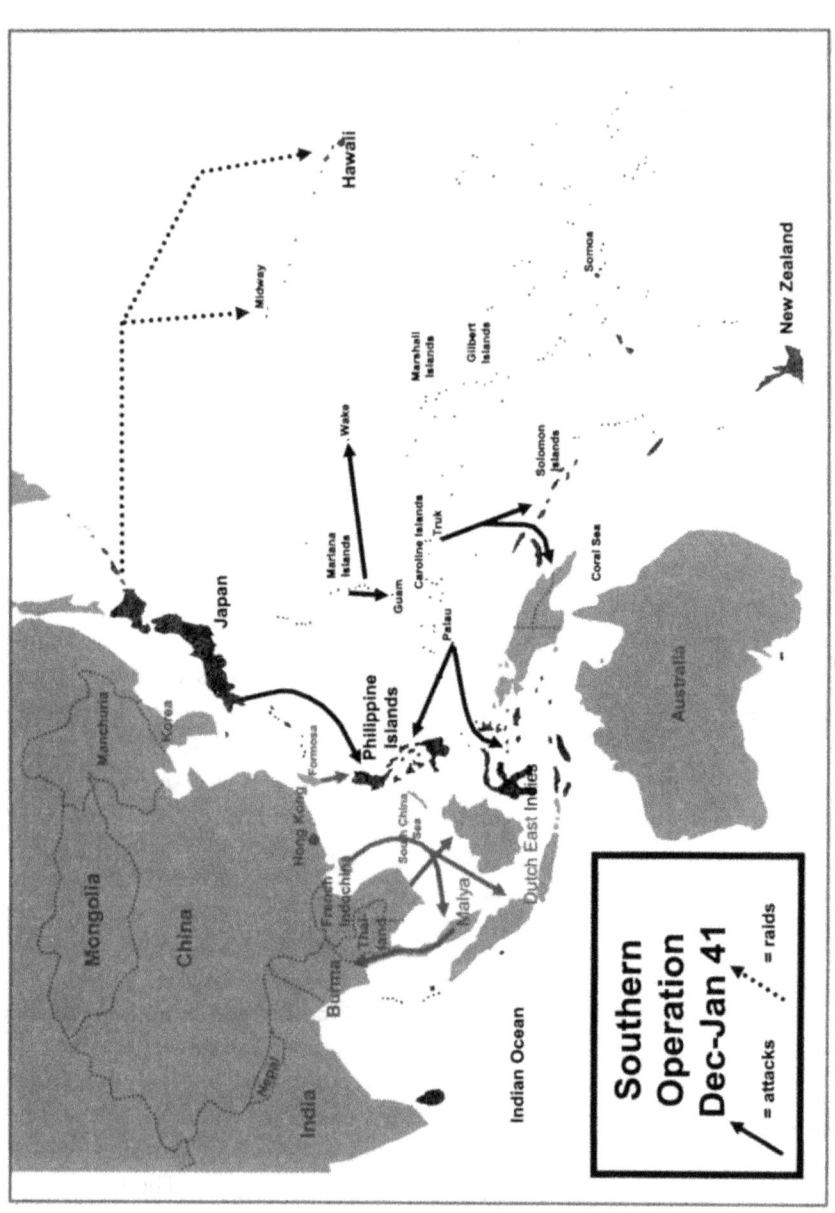

Figure 53.

commander of the air group responsible for leading the aircrews throughout training and would be the onsite commander during the actual raid. Fuchida had been Genda's classmate at the military academy, and the two had remained friends ever since. Fuchida was known as one of the best high-level bomber pilots in the Japanese navy, but his leadership was the key to him being selected to command. Fuchida was an outstanding combat leader, levelheaded and cool in critical situations, but he was selected to command because he was able to convey the detailed plans from the staff into maneuvers that the energetic aircrews could execute. Fuchida was told what tasks the aircrews needed to be able to accomplish without being told of the plan. It was not until late September that Genda briefed Fuchida on the details of the plan.

In early September the Imperial General Staff briefed the emperor on war preparations, usually a formality because the emperor listened at these meetings and never said a word. However, Hirohito spoke up at this meeting, warning his military officers not to forgo negotiations as a way to avoid war. He emphasized that the Foreign Ministry would continue to negotiate with the United States and its Allies to try to solve the disagreement peacefully, and that the military should not do anything to hamper the discussions.

By late September two new aircraft carriers, composing the 5th Carrier Division, joined the First Air Fleet. *Shokaku* was completed on 7 August, and *Zuikaku* joined the fleet on 24 September. Their air wings had been formed before the ships were completed and had been training, and they now joined their ships. The 4th Carrier Division was transferred to other fleets, and the 5th Carrier Division was added to the First Air Fleet, meaning that Operation *HAWAII* now had six first-line aircraft carriers.

While the First Air Fleet continued to work on the air attack of Pearl Harbor, Yamamoto added another method of attack to the operation—submarines. In the end, 27 of Japan's 63 submarines would take part in Operation *HAWAII*. Yamamoto wanted the submarines to participate to accomplish four tasks:

- Reconnaissance.
- Attacking ships leaving Pearl Harbor during and after the air attack.
- Protecting the First Air Fleet from any US surface fleet.
- Picking up downed flyers that could not make it back to the carriers.

Additionally, the 6th Fleet (the submarine fleet) was tasked to create a Special Attack Force, five submarines that would carry midget submarines to Pearl Harbor. Japan had used midget submarines before, but these were launched from surface ships. The Japanese modified fleet submarines to carry the midget submarines to within 10 miles of Pearl Harbor where they would be launched to enter the harbor and attack American warships. The midget submarines were 78 feet long, weighed 46 tons, were armed with two torpedoes, had a crew of two, and had a range of 80 miles surfaced and 18 submerged. The air planners were distressed by the addition of submarines to their plans. They thought the chance of one of the submarines being spotted was excessive and would cause the entire raid to lose the element of surprise, deemed key by the air planners. Yamamoto listened to his airmen, but in the end he decided to maintain the submarines as part of the operation.

From 11 to 15 September the leaders of the Japanese navy gathered at the Naval Staff College to participate in the annual naval exercise, a command post exercise conducted in the buildings of the college. In a closely guarded secret room, Yamamoto gathered all of the officers who were aware of Operation *HAWAII* for a separate war game. From 11 to 14 September Yamamoto participated in the exercise based on the Southern Operation. The different fleets conducted the operations they had been tasked to accomplish during the Southern Operation. For the most part, the exercise determined that that part of the plan was sound; only minor modifications were made.

On 15 September Yamamoto, closely watched by the representatives of the naval general staff, exercised Operation *HAWAII*. After discussions (some times heated) about which route to sail, the fleet, and preattack aerial reconnaissance, the exercise began. In the first iteration American reconnaissance aircraft located the Japanese fleet, resulting in the aircrews having to fight their way to the target and only causing minor damage to the US fleet. American bombers followed the Japanese planes back to their carriers where they sank two Japanese carriers and damaged two. A review of the action determined that the fleet had sailed too far south and had arrived at the launch point too early. The planners modified their plan and conducted another iteration in which the Americans did not spot the Japanese until the planes were over their targets. The Japanese destroyed two American carriers, four battleships, and three cruisers and damaged one carrier, one battleship, and three cruisers. Additionally, most of the American aircraft were destroyed. However, the few remaining American aircraft were able to locate the fleet and sink a Japanese carrier, a fact not lost on Nagumo who determined a quick escape from the area was key to his operations.

The day after the exercise, the participants gathered to discuss the exercise. The "American" and Japanese commanders briefed, as did the umpires. All agreed that the fleet had to sail a northerly route to avoid detection. They determined they had to arrive 450 miles from Hawaii at sunset because all American scout planes would be returning to base at that time, thus allowing the fleet to sail to the launch point undetected. Satisfied with the exercise, Yamamoto gathered the participants for a dinner that night, but he still did not have the naval general staff's permission to conduct Operation *HAWAII*.

The Foreign Ministry continued negotiations with the United States, but it was really an exercise in futility. The United States demanded that Japan leave French Indochina and China before trade resumed, while the Japanese demanded the resumption of trade as the catalyst for other agreements. The two sides were irreversibly divided, but negotiations continued. As dialogue with the Americans faltered, the cabinet ministry contrived to get Japan on a wartime footing. On 15 October the prime minister and all of his cabinet resigned to allow the country to form a new "war" government. Hirohito, on the advice of his advisers, selected ex-War Minister Hideki Tojo, an active duty army general, as the new prime minister. Tojo formed a cabinet with members he could control and also assumed the duties of war minister and army chief of staff. Japan now had a de facto military dictator, and any hope of a peaceful solution was over.

For the next month, the First Air Fleet refined its procedures while the naval general staff debated the merits of Operation *HAWAII*. Some on the staff considered the plan a gamble: how could six aircraft carriers sneak across the Pacific Ocean and attack the major US base without being detected? Others thought the assets earmarked for Hawaii could be better used in the Southern Operation. After all the Southern Operation was the main effort, and Operation *HAWAII* was a secondary effort. Yamamoto was convinced that the operation was imperative if Japan hoped to win any war with the United States. Therefore, on 17 October he sent one of his most trusted staff officers, Captain Kameto Kuroshima, to Tokyo to get a decision from the naval general staff. Kuroshima was no stranger to the naval general staff, having been dispatched by Yamamoto numerous times to brief it. Kuroshima briefed the merits of the plan one more time, but with each point he made, the staff responded by criticizing the plan.

Finally, Kuroshima played the trump card Yamamoto gave him.

Kuroshima informed the naval general staff that if Operation *HAWAII* was not approved, Yamamoto could no longer guarantee Japan's security, and he, therefore, would be compelled to resign. The staff officers could not believe their ears, but they did not want to risk losing the best admiral in the navy. They therefore approved the plan's implementation if Japan went to war, as long as Yamamoto promised to make the carriers available to the Southern Operation as soon as possible after the attack. Yamamoto and his staff had meticulously planned for nine months, and now they had permission to conduct their operation, convinced that it was Japan's best hope for defeating America.

During early November Japanese preparations accelerated as war became certain. Fuchida and the air planners completed their plan based on the war games. On 2 November Nagumo briefed all of the senior commanders (ship captains and carrier air group commanders) on the plan to attack the US fleet in Pearl Harbor. The First Air Fleet conducted full rehearsals of the attack on 3 to 6 November, with full after-action reviews and modifications to the plan based on events. Also on 6 November the Combined Fleet published Combined Fleet Order #1, which explained the entire plan (the Southern Operation and Operation *HAWAII*) from the initial attacks until the defensive perimeter was established. Events continued to transpire quickly.

The submarines began departing Japan on 11 November when the 3d Squadron sailed and was followed on 16 and 18 November by additional squadrons of submarines. All submarines proceeded to Japanese anchorages en route to refuel and were in position around Hawaii by 6 December. Throughout November, ships assigned to Operation *HAWAII* slowly slipped away from their home ports for the assembly point of Hitokappu Bay in the Kuril Islands. The Japanese intended to assemble the fleet in an isolated anchorage without drawing attention. By 22 November the fleet was assembled, and Nagumo briefed the operation to all of the subordinate commanders. He and his staff detailed the route they would sail, the plan of attack, contingencies if the fleet was spotted, logistics, etc. Yamamoto sent instructions to Nagumo on 24 November informing him that the fleet would sail the next day. The First Air Fleet, now renamed the Pearl Harbor Attack Force, lifted anchor and set sail on 25 November. Nagumo still did not have his attack orders; the diplomats were still trying. Nagumo would receive the attack order en route if negotiations failed.

The 30 ships of the Pearl Harbor Attack Force formed up and headed east led by the cruiser *Abukuma*, followed by four destroyers, the battleships

Fuchida Chart

	Plane Type	Carrier	# Planned/Launched	Armament	Target
First Wave  CDR Mitsuo Fuchido Launch 0600-0615	Kate (High Level) 	Akagi Kaga Soryu Hiryu	15/15 15/14 10/10 10/10 } 49	One 1,750-lb armor-piercing bomb	Battleships
	Kate (Torpedo)	Akagi Kaga Soryu Hiryu	12/12 12/12 8/8 8/8 } 40	One 1,750-lb aerial torpedo	Battleships Cruisers
	Val Dive Bomber 	Shokaku Zuikaku	27/26 27/25 } 51	One 550-lb bomb	Ford Island, Hickam and Wheeler Air Bases
	Zero Fighter 	Akagi Kaga Soryu Hiryu Shokaku Zuikaku	9/9 9/9 9/8 6/6 6/5 6/6 } 43	Two 20 mm cannons Two 7.7 mm MGs	Ford Island Air Base Hickam Air Base Wheeler Air Base Ewa Air Base Kaneohe Air Base
			189/183		
Second Wave LCDR Shigekazu Shimazaki Launch 0715-0730	Kate (High Level)	Zuikaku Shokaku	27/27 27/27 } 54	Two 550-lb bombs or One 550-lb bomb and six 132-lb bombs	Ford Island, Hickam and Kaneohe Air Bases
	Val Dive Bomber 	Soryu Hiryu Akagi Kaga	18/17 18/17 18/18 27/26 } 78	One 550-lb bomb	Cruisers Battleships Destroyers
	Zero Fighter 	Akagi Kaga Soryu Hiryu	9/9 9/9 9/9 9/8 } 35	Two 20 mm cannons Two 7.7 mm MGs	Ford Island Air Base Hickam Air Base Wheeler Air Base Kaneohe Air Base
			171/167		
			360/350		

Figure 54.

Hiei and *Kirishima*, which led the six carriers flanked by destroyers. The cruisers *Tone* and *Chikuma* flanked the formation while three submarines brought up the rear, ready to move forward to scout ahead. As the fleet steamed toward Pearl Harbor, the destroyers had to refuel everyday in the stormy seas of the northern route, losing sailors overboard during one operation.

On 1 December the cabinet met with the emperor in the Imperial Palace, and the decision was made that Japan had to declare war on the United States, Great Britain, and the Netherlands. The naval general staff informed Yamamoto, and on 2 December he gave a warning order to all of his subordinate fleet commanders telling them the exact date and time of their attacks would be sent on a later date. On 2 December Yamamoto received a message from the naval general staff, "Climb Mount Niitaka 1208." The coded message meant the war would begin on 8 December (7 December Hawaiian time). Diplomacy had failed and Japan would attack the United States, Great Britain, and the Netherlands.

On 4 December the three tankers of Supply Group 2 refueled the task force and left formation to a linkup point where they would rendezvous with the task force during its return. On 6 December the four tankers of Supply Group 1 refueled all of the ships, and they too broke off to rendezvous with the fleet during its withdrawal. While the ships of the Pearl Harbor Attack Force refueled for the last time before the attack, Tojo cabled his ambassador to the United States, retired Admiral Kichisaburo Nomura, and informed him to be prepared to receive a 14-part message that had to be delivered to the United States before 0800, 7 December.

Once the tankers had departed, Nagumo raised the flag signal that Admiral Togo had raised before the Battle of Tsushima Straights: "The rise and fall of the Empire depends upon this battle: everyone will do his duty with utmost effort." The fleet, now unencumbered by the slow tankers, increased speed to 24 knots to race to the launch point. The last day of peace the United States would enjoy for the next 3½ years was 6 December 1941.

III. Suggested Route and Vignettes

Introduction

The attack on Pearl Harbor occurred over two hours on 7 December 1941. The Japanese attacked six major military installations all across Oahu that morning, leaving death and destruction in their wake. This guide is designed to examine the entire attack during a one-day visit. To accomplish this, an early start is required. Only two of the six major installations attacked that morning will be visited on this staff ride; the other four will be discussed at other locations.

The first couple of stands will discuss the antagonists' preparations, and the last stands discuss the repercussions of the United States' failings and Japan's successes. The route of this guide follows no "tour" signs; therefore, the staff ride leader should recon the route before the staff ride and should have a detailed road map. Most of the stands are on active military installations, so be careful not to stray into off-limits areas.

The staff group leader may want to start this staff ride at a location where he or she can discuss the overview of the attack (Part II of this guide). Locations for this stand may be the Aiea Bay State Recreation Area picnic area (the first stand of the staff ride is in the same location but by the water looking at Pearl Harbor). This information may be covered the day or night before the ride in a briefing format.

Map to Stands 1-3

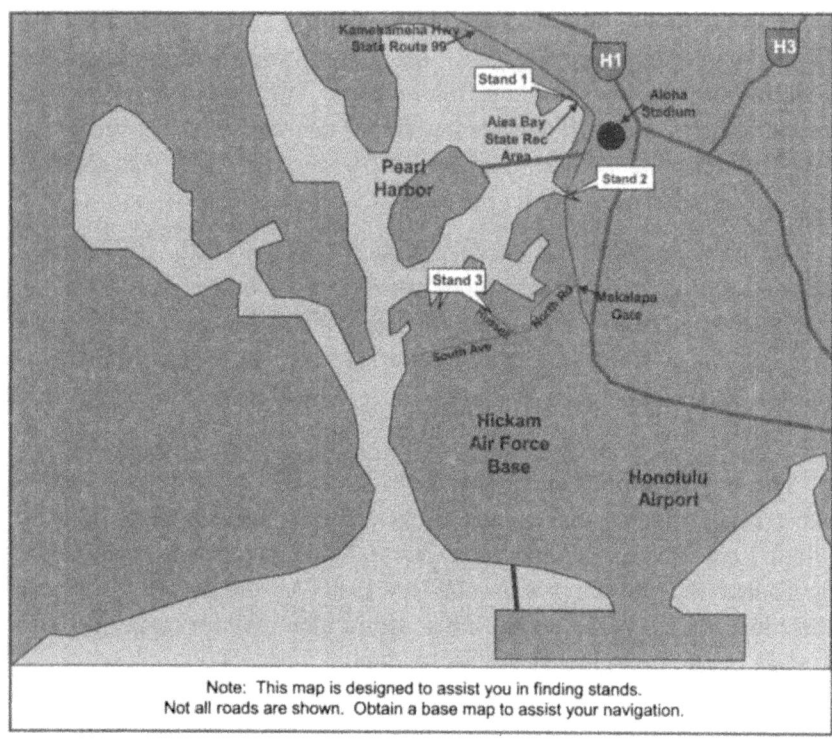

Note: This map is designed to assist you in finding stands.
Not all roads are shown. Obtain a base map to assist your navigation.

Map to
Stands 4-7

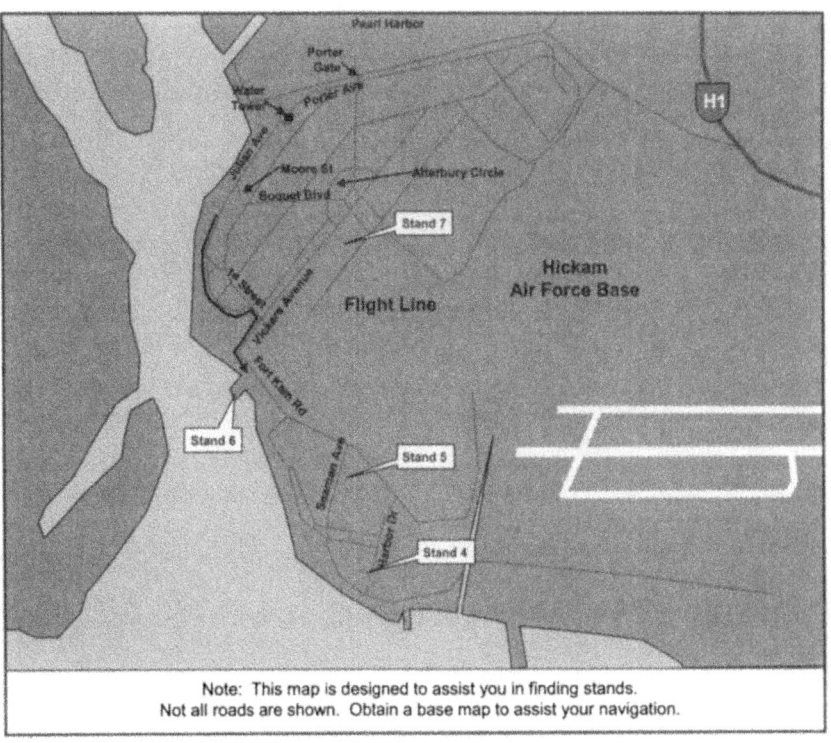

Map to
Stands 8-10

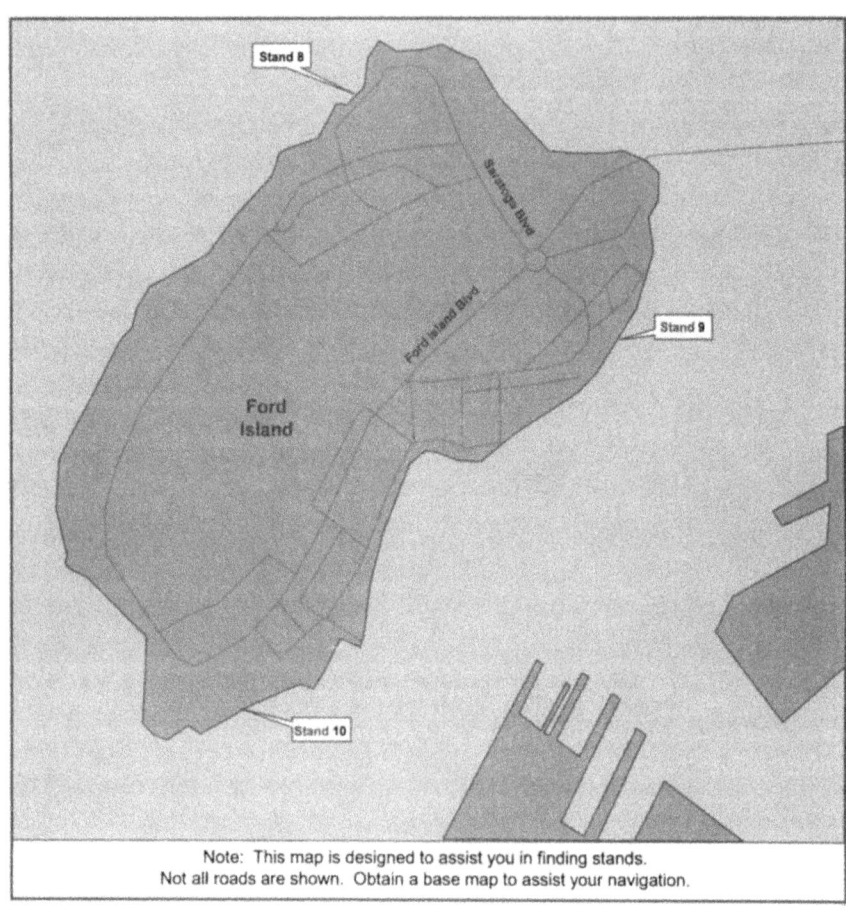

Stand 1
Japanese Espionage

Directions: The first stand is conducted at Aiea Bay State Recreation Area. From Kamehameha Highway (State Route 99) turn onto McGrew Loop. Make an immediate left at the "Aiea Bay State Recreation Area" sign. Park in the parking lot. If you plan to conduct an overview, move to the vicinity of the picnic area. When the overview is complete, move to the edge of the water where you can see Pearl Harbor.

Orientation: You are standing in the Aiea State Recreation Area. Today, any person can stand here and observe the activities in Pearl Harbor just as the Japanese spies did in 1941. The East Loch is the water to your front, the location where the destroyers berthed. Ford Island is directly across the loch, and the battleship is the USS *Missouri*, which is moored just fore of the USS *Arizona* on Battleship Row. The northwest side of Ford Island is where the aircraft carriers usually berthed.

Description: If the Japanese had any hope of crippling the US Pacific Fleet, they had to have extremely accurate intelligence on the ships of the fleet, the anchorage, and the other bases on Oahu that could influence any attack. Hawaii had a large Japanese population, both US citizens of Japanese descent and expatriates, who had always been a security concern for the United States. The Japanese government maintained a consulate 7 miles from Pearl Harbor (it is still there) and had been using consulate personnel to observe US military activity for some time. When the Pacific Fleet transferred to Pearl Harbor in 1940, the Japanese government told Consul General Kiichi Gunji to send periodic reports on naval activity in Hawaii. Gunji selected the consulate's treasurer, Kohichi Seki, to accomplish the task because he had attended the Naval Academy at Eta Jima before being discharged for medical reasons. The Honolulu newspapers published the schedule of fleet movements, and Seki simply rode a cab around Pearl Harbor to verify the newspaper accounts. As Seki continued his observations, he realized that the Pacific Fleet was extremely predictable; part of the fleet would depart on Monday and be back in port on Friday or Saturday. The Pacific Fleet was usually in port on Sundays.

As planning for Operation *HAWAII* progressed, the Japanese Consulate received a new employee, Tadashi Morimura, to assist with processing dual-nationality citizens. In fact, Morimura was actually Takeo Yoshikawa, a trained intelligence agent of the naval general staff. Yoshikawa was a graduate of Eta Jima who had been discharged from the Navy because of illness. He had extensive knowledge of the US Navy, and upon his discharge, the naval general staff's intelligence division sent him to school to improve his English, and trained him on the US Pacific Fleet. Yoshikawa arrived in Honolulu on 27 March 1941 and was immediately assigned one of the consulate's bungalows and a car with driver, actions that seemed odd to the other members of the consulate staff.

Yoshikawa started his reconnaissance soon after his arrival. He selected several locations where he could observe Pearl Harbor, including Aiea. He soon confirmed the previous observation that the Pacific Fleet was usually in port on Sundays. As he became comfortable with his operations at Pearl Harbor, Yoshikawa began observing the other military installations on Oahu. He knew of the Naval Air Station (NAS) at Kaneohe, but he could not get close enough from the road to make accurate observations. He therefore decided to rent a boat, and using maids from the consulate as cover, anchored his "party" boat off the coast at Kaneohe and observed from there. When he had difficulty viewing Wheeler Field, he attended the Wheeler Field Open House on 6 August and was allowed to freely roam around the field. The only restriction was against taking pictures.

The airfields were the most difficult locations to observe, but the Japanese needed accurate information, so Yoshikawa continued to use the tourist cover. Taking one of the women employees of the consulate as his date, Yoshikawa rented an airplane and flew around all the different installations. Restrictions prevented him from overflying each installation, but observing the targets from the air allowed him to gather all the required information. At each airfield he was able to gather information on the runways, hangars, facilities, aircraft, and defenses. At Pearl Harbor he observed Ford Island NAS and the ships in anchorage. As Yoshikawa continued the routine of his espionage, he made another discovery that would be invaluable to attack planners. He noticed that US reconnaissance aircraft concentrated their searches south of Oahu. Yoshikawa was able to clearly view every major military installation and assess US forces' exploitable patterns, and he forwarded that information to the naval general staff in Japan.

Based on Yoshikawa's information, the naval general staff decided to recon the Pearl Harbor Attack Force's planned sailing route. Normal shipping between Japan and the United States was suspended, but an agreement between the countries allowed limited sailings to repatriate citizens from one country to the other. On 23 October 1941 *Tatuta Maru* arrived in Honolulu with two intelligence agents aboard who carried instructions for the consulate and a supply of radios for civilian spies who were in place on Oahu in case the United States closed the consulate. The second ship, *Taiyo Maru*, arrived in Honolulu on 22 October, having sailed the exact route the attack force planned to use. The two intelligence agents aboard observed no other vessels on the route and learned that the US aerial screen line only extended 200 miles north of Oahu. The *Taiyo Maru* arrived in harbor at 0830, the planned time of attack, so the agents could observe conditions on Oahu at the scheduled time of attack.

Before the attack, Japan had developed an extensive collection plan for all of the information required to precisely plan an attack on the Pacific Fleet. The planners knew about each of the airfields and the aircraft assigned to each, which allowed the planners to properly assign assets to each target. They knew the exact location where ships berthed so the planners could select appropriate routes with the appropriate assets to attack each target. In short, the Japanese had excellent intelligence from which to plan their attack.

Vignette: In 1943 the counterintelligence section of Fourteenth Naval District's Intelligence Office published an analysis of espionage problems in Hawaii:

> From the facts at hand, it must be said that almost all military and naval information known to have been transmitted from Hawaii to Japan, either by Consulate or agents sent here on special missions, was gathered by the simple expedient of open observation, without trespassing restricted areas.... In only a few instances were Consulate observers known to have used binoculars to observe Pearl Harbor and the Naval Air Station Kaneohe Bay, and even then, not illegally.... Accurate maps and charts of the Hawaiian Islands and adjacent waters long were on sale in downtown Honolulu, and available to any purchaser. Tourist maps showed the approximate location of many military and naval installations. Photographs of many strategic places on Oahu were on sale in Honolulu stores-even panoramic views of Pearl Harbor.... Unless vigorous, astute, and coordinated counter-espionage measures are placed in operation in Hawaii, the primary task of Counter-intelligence-denial of information to the enemy-will never be performed.

(*Hearings Before the Joint Committee on the Investigation of the Pearl Harbor Attack*, Congress of the United States, Seventy-Ninth Congress, Washington DC, 1946, part 35, 556-57, 572, hereafter cited as *IPHA*.)

Teaching point 1. Counterespionage. In a free society, how can we prevent an enemy from conducting reconnaissance of a target if that enemy does not overtly break any laws?

As the staff ride leader leads this discussion, there are a few topics to consider. If a person is not breaking a law, you can not stop them. However, have the students consider:

    a. If a person is a foreign national, reports of suspicious activity may lead to a professional counterespionage agency observing that person more closely.

    b. There are steps we can take to make information gathering more difficult: watch what is posted on websites or is commercially available, understand where an installation is vulnerable to legal observation, and mitigate any possible damage from that location.

    c. Altering defensive measures (shifting "Jersey barriers," access points) makes reconnaissance less effective.

Teaching point 2. Predictability. Did the Pacific Fleet pattern of sailing on Mondays and returning on Saturdays give the enemy an edge?

The staff ride leader can have the students discuss US failures by developing a pattern that the enemy exploited (always being in port on Sunday, always focusing aerial screens to the south). Once the discussion lags, ask them, "How do you prevent predictability?" Issues here may include constant use of the same route, unchanged entrance procedures to a facility, lax and unaltered security procedures (like airport security screening before 11 September), etc.

Stand 2
Homeland Defense

Directions: Retrace your route back to Kamehameha Highway (State Route 99). Turn right on Kamehameha Highway (State Route 99) heading toward Pearl Harbor. Turn into the USS *Arizona* Memorial parking lot, and turn left at the bottom of the hill. Pull the vehicle as far south as you can (parking may be difficult here). Dismount and walk until you can observe the Kamehameha Highway bridge over Halawa Stream.

Orientation: In 1941 this bridge was designated the "New Kam Highway Bridge over Halawa Stream" in the Hawaiian Department's standing operating procedures (SOP). It was one of 19 highway bridges the Hawaiian Department ordered to be guarded in the event of any alert. The 25th Infantry Division was responsible for this bridge and was guarding it on 7 December 1941.

Description: In 1941, 37 percent of Hawaii's population was Japanese; 24 percent was Caucasian; 15 perecent was Hawaiian; and the remainder was mixed among Filipino, Chinese, Puerto Rican, and Korean. With such a large percentage of Japanese people living in Hawaii, the military was extremely concerned about sabotage. As such, it designated crucial civilian infrastructure for protection. In its SOP, the Hawaiian Department ordered numerous civilian facilities to be guarded during any alert. Those facilities included 51 railroad bridges, 19 highway bridges, five telephone exchanges, eight electric substations, one cold storage plant, four water pumping stations, and one radio station. Both the 24th and 25th Infantry Divisions developed their own SOPs that required their subordinate units to occupy defensive positions in case of attack by military forces and required protection for these critical locations (see figure 55).

When the Hawaiian National Guard was federalized in October 1940, the territorial governor was left with a void of military strength for his own use. Realizing it was his responsibility to guard the key facilities that the US Army was guarding, the governor passed a law creating the Hawaiian Territorial Home Guard, a militia organization that would replace the federalized National Guard. Unfortunately, the Hawaiian Territorial Home Guard had not been organized by 7 December 1941.

LTG Short was concerned about protecting the citizens of Oahu in case of attack. In March 1941 he published, in conjunction with local civilian governments, a plan to protect Oahu's civilian population in case of bombardment. The extensive plan detailed how the city of Honolulu

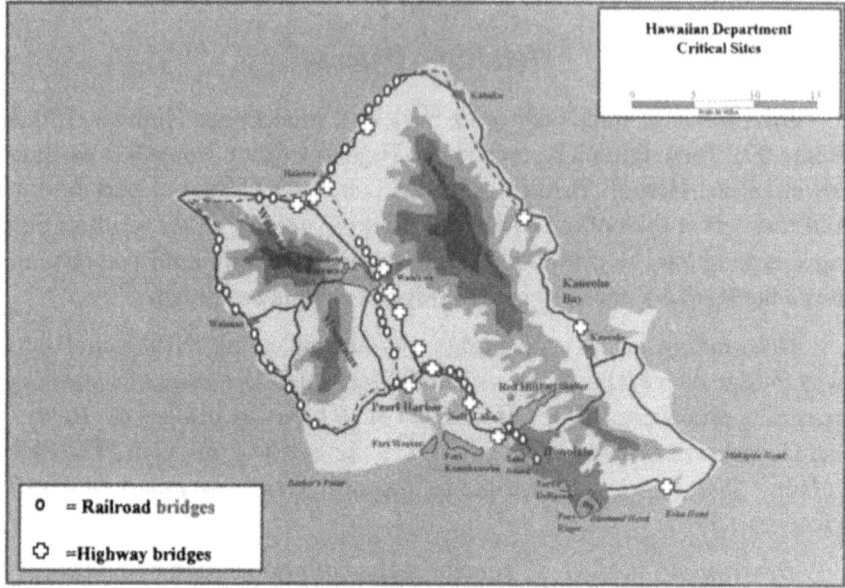

Figure 55.

and Oahu's territorial government would protect its citizens in case of an attack. The plan included sections on organization, air raid protection, evacuation, and use of workers.

In the event of attack, Honolulu would use the police and fire departments to deal with the situation initially. Then, a "General Committee," consisting of the mayor, a secretary, representatives of the Hawaiian Department and 14th Naval District, FBI, and chairmen of appointed subcommittees, would deal with the emergency. The subcommittees, headed by an appropriate official and with members from key organizations, would manage specific problems. The subcommittees follow.

Subcommittee	Chairman	Duties
Law Enforcement	Chief of Police	Patrolling Prison camps Traffic control Blackout enforcement
Relief	Red Cross Chairman	Food rationing Billeting Medical aid Casualty reporting
Damage Control	City Chief Engineer	Fire protection Clear ruins Construct defense works Bury the dead
Procurement	City & County Purchasing Agent	Food preparation Fuel maintenance Purchase supplies
Finance	City and County Comptroller	Control expenditures Emergency budget preparation
Legislative	City and County Attorney	Prepare legislation Special court establishment Emergency labor laws
Public Relations and Publicity	Not mentioned	Morale Publicity Public education

Additional civilian subcommittees (advisory groups) were also planned. These included housing, food, transportation, labor, publicity, engineering, medical, and damage control.

Civilian protection from air attack was a major concern, so the officials extensively planned to protect the citizens from the air. Hawaii was divided into districts and divisions that contained medical support, chemical protection, rescue teams, and collection stations. The plan detailed diagrams and descriptions of shelters civilians could construct and maps to large, government shelters. In case of attack, officials wanted to evacuate all nonessential personnel to reduce casualties. The plan had locations (with the number of personnel the facility could accommodate) and a comprehensive transportation plan.

The planners realized extensive labor would be needed after an attack and planned to use 20,000 workers to assist in any recovery and in defensive preparation. The plan detailed "bed-down" locations for the workers and a general plan of requirements; detailed plans would be developed based on the situation. However, this effort ensured a ready pool of skilled workers prepared to provide any support that was needed.

Vignette: On 23 December 1941 Hawaii Governor J.W. Poindexter reflected on the plan to protect citizens in a letter to Hawaiian Department Commander LTG Walter Short: "The citizens of the Hawaiian Islands have always appreciated that these Islands were important to National Defense from a military standpoint, but it has been only since your arrival in these Islands on February 5, 1941 that it has been brought home to the civil population the importance of the part it would play in the event of a war in the Pacific. On December 7th, the citizens of these Islands met the hour of their test in such a manner as to make me proud to be the Chief Executive of these Islands. Your foresight in urging the population to prepare to meet the possible vicissitudes of war and the joint efforts of the Army and civil population in planning and preparing for this emergency was magnificently rewarded." (*IPHA*, part 24, 1,932.)

Teaching point 1. Critical site defense. How extensively have we planned to defend civilian and military sites that are critical to military operations around our home bases?

The staff ride leader should get the students to discuss how prepared their units are to deal with an attack at their own installations. Before 11 September this seemed impossible, but now posts and units must be prepared to defend themselves at home. Ask the students what the critical locations are on and around their posts or bases and about the plan to defend them.

Teaching point 2. Civil defense. How extensively have our cities planned for civil defense?

Honolulu had a meticulous plan for dealing with an attack, and on 7 December, they were able to successfully respond to the Japanese attack. Fire units were quickly dispatched to fight fires and handle destruction, civilians were evacuated, work parties were quickly formed, and a blackout was quickly initiated and enforced, due largely to having a good plan on the shelf. Have the students discuss how well they think our citizens and towns are prepared for another attack. More important, have them discuss their responsibility for civil defense.

Stand 3
American Intelligence

Directions: Depart the USS *Arizona* Memorial parking lot and turn right on Kamehameha Highway (State Route 99). Enter Pearl Harbor Naval Base through the Makalapa Gate (security police will check your vehicle for Department of Defense stickers and check each person's identification). Once through the gate, turn left on North Road. At the Nimitz Gate, North Road becomes South Avenue. From the Nimitz Gate, drive 0.8 miles on South Avenue and turn right on Russell Avenue. Drive 0.4 miles (go straight at the Stop sign) and park near the two-story building with long, exterior balconies on the right. Conduct the stand in the grass in front of the building.

Orientation: This is Building 1 at Pearl Harbor, the Naval Shipyard Administration Building. In 1941 the Combat Intelligence Unit (CIU), commanded by Commander Joseph Rochefort, was located in this building. Rochefort and CIU determined that Japan was going to attack Midway in 1942, which allowed the United States to ambush and win the decisive Battle of Midway. (Hal Holbrook played Rochefort in the 1976 movie, "Midway.") Ford Island is 300 meters to the north, and Hickam Air Force Base is to the south.

Description: The American authorities knew the Japanese were conducting espionage all over Oahu, but there was nothing they could do to stop it. The FBI, the Navy District Intelligence Office (DIO), Hawaiian Department G2, and the Honolulu police all had learned of the consulate activities and observed the Japanese as they gathered their information, but since the Japanese were not overtly breaking the law, they could not stop them. These counterintelligence professionals let the Japanese know they knew they were conducting espionage in an attempt to intimidate them, would talk to them as they departed the consulate grounds, and let them know they were following them.

The counterintelligence agencies were able to get some wiretaps on a few phones in the consulate, but they concentrated on the senior members who were not involved in spying, so they did not gain any intelligence from the taps. In hope of determining what information the Japanese were passing to Tokyo, the DIO attempted to get copies of the cables sent from the consulate, but the telegraph companies would not violate the Federal Communications Act of 1934 that prohibited intercepting messages to and from a foreign country. While the counterintelligence agencies were unable to stop Japanese intelligence gathering, other government agencies were having success in determining Japan's intentions; the United States was reading Japan's diplomatic traffic.

The Japanese had developed a series of codes for their diplomats to use. The most secure and the one the Japanese most trusted was termed "Purple." This was a system that used a combination of machinery and ciphers to secure message traffic and was so intricate that the Japanese were convinced that it could not be broken. The problem for the Japanese was that the United States had broken it in August 1940 and had been reading its most important diplomatic traffic ever since. The US Army Signal Intelligence Service hired the best cryptologists, spent 18 months working on the problem, and was eventually successful. The Japanese used other, less secure codes (mainly, the J-series codes) that the United States also broke. The information gathered from all of the diplomatic codes was called "Magic" intelligence. The US Army and Navy synergistically cooperated on Magic, with the Army concentrating on Purple while the Navy concentrated on the J series.

On the surface, Magic seemed like a great advantage for the United States, but it had many problems. Purple messages only contained information the foreign office wanted its diplomats to know, and often it was better if the diplomats in the United States did not know much. There were only eight Purple decrypting machines in existence, and the United States had to thoughtfully decide who should have them. In the end, four were placed in Washington (two for the Army, two for the Navy), three were provided to the British Allies, and the last was given to General Douglas MacArthur, commander, US Armed Forces Far East, in the Philippines. Hawaii did not have its own machine and depended on Washington for Magic information.

The Japanese sent an average of 26 messages a day using the Purple code, which caused difficulties for the US code breakers because it took up to a week to decode each message. Once decoded, the message had to go to another office to be translated, and due to an acute shortage of qualified Japanese linguists, it could take another week to translate any message. It could take up to 14 days before intelligence officers had the message in their hands.

The US intelligence experts had to decide carefully who could be exposed to Magic intelligence. If too many people knew of Magic information, the Japanese could determine that the Purple code was broken and they could change the code. Therefore, the Army only allowed the Secretary of War, the Chief of Staff, the Chief of War Plans, and the G2 to be exposed to "Magic." The Navy only allowed access to the Secretary of the Navy, the Chief of Naval Operations (CNO), the Chief of War Plans, and the Chief of Intelligence. The president had access to Magic, but even this was stopped for a while when a copy of a Magic message was found in his military secretary's trash. Each service issued general guidance to their subordinates based on Magic but were very careful to conceal the source, which sometimes led to very simple information being delivered to commanders when more detailed information was available.

While intelligence units in Washington were reading the diplomatic traffic, the CIU was reading the Japanese navy's "flag officer's" code, the most secure naval code that was used to pass critical naval communications. The CIU had cracked the code in 1926 and had been reading it ever since. Unfortunately, on 1 December 1940 the Japanese changed the flag officer's code, and the CIU could not break the new code until after the United States was thrust into the war. The CIU would, however, break the code again, which provided information that was instrumental in the overwhelming American victory at Midway.

Despite being able to read many of the Japanese codes, the Navy's senior leaders were affected by a power struggle between the Chief of War Plans and the Chief of Intelligence. Each organization wanted to produce the data on Japanese intentions based on intelligence gathered by all sources. This in-fighting produced nothing but mistrust and poor information for the Navy's senior commanders.

Despite the troubles and tribulations of gaining Magic, the intercepts did provide the United States with some critical information. On 24 September 1941 (message not decoded and translated until 9 October) the Japanese sent detailed instructions on how to report the locations of ships in Pearl Harbor to the consulate in Honolulu using a detailed grid system (this is known as the "bomb plot" message). Army intelligence analysts considered the message significant, but senior leaders did not and never forwarded any information about it to LTG Short, the Hawaiian Department commander. Navy senior leaders considered the message interesting but not critical and ordered the information passed to the Pacific and Asiatic Fleets. For unknown reasons Admiral Kimmel never received the message, but Washington assumed he had.

On 15 November 1941 (message not decoded and translated until 3 December) the Japanese consulate was ordered to make reports on Pearl Harbor twice a week and to alter the times they sent each report. Washington decided not to send this information to the commanders in Hawaii.

On 29 November 1941 the Japanese Foreign Ministry sent a message to all if its embassies and consulates around the world with a series of code words that would be broadcast on Japanese open shortwave radio networks during the weather report indicating when diplomatic relations were going to be severed, a step just short of war. There were codes for severing relations with the USSR, England, and the United States. The code for cutting relations with the United States was "East Wind Rain," so the message became known as the "winds message." Again, this information was never passed to Kimmel and Short, nor were they informed when one of the codes was heard on 3 December.

On 6 December 1941 the code breakers intercepted a message to the Washington embassy telling them to be prepared to receive a 14-part message that had to be delivered to the US State Department by 1300, 7 December (0800 Hawaiian time). When the message came in, the US code breakers were able to decrypt it and translate it faster than the Japanese embassy, and when Roosevelt read it, he supposedly said, "This means war." (Popular lore says this message was a declaration of war. In fact, it was a reply to a previous message the United States sent. While the message "meant war," it was not itself a declaration of war.) When Army Chief of Staff General George C. Marshall saw the message, he ordered war warnings to be sent to all commands. The Army Staff sent messages to all subordinate commanders, but atmospheric conditions prevented it from sending the message to the Hawaiian Department. The officer responsible for sending the message could have asked the Navy to send the message but instead decided to send it by civilian telegraph. The message arrived in Honolulu at 0733, 7 December and did not arrive at Fort Shafter (Hawaiian Department headquarters) until 1145. It was not decoded and into Short's hands until 1458.

Vignette: The counterintelligence agents' frustration is apparent in Rear Admiral Theodore S. Wilkinson's testimony to the Hart Commission in 1944. Wilkinson, who was a commander and Director, Office of Naval Intelligence, in December 1941, testified: "It would also be indicated similarly elsewhere, but the fact that a comprehensive espionage was being carried on was, I think, known through the district intelligence officers to the naval commanders in all of these ports, and I know that the time I was in Hawaii, that we were cognizant of that fact, and we were helpless to stop it. We could not censor their mails. We could not censor the dispatches. We could not prevent the taking of photographs. We could not arrest Japanese suspects. There was nothing we could do to stop it, and all hands knew that espionage was going on all along, and reports were going back to Japan." (*IPHA*, part 4, 1,841).

Teaching point 1. Freedom versus security. Do laws like the Federal Communications Act of 1934, which are passed to secure our freedom, in fact make the nation less safe?

The staff ride leader should get students to compare and contrast laws that secure our freedom and laws that limit freedoms but maintain security. As the discussion continues, inject the Patriot Act and ask students if the loss of certain civil liberties is worth the protection gained.

Teaching point 2. Language skills. How did a lack of skilled linguists affect the Americans' ability to gather intelligence?

Due to this shortage, critical messages could take a week to translate. Ask students if our nation is better off today. (On 28 September 2004 the *New York Times* reported that 120,000 hours of potentially valuable terrorism-related recordings have not been translated due to a shortage of skilled linguists in the FBI.) Ask students how we can improve our language capability.

Teaching point 3. Dissemination. What good is having great intelligence if you cannot share it with the commanders who need it?

Have students discuss how to keep sources and methods secret while still being able to provide information to those who really need it. The staff ride leader can also discuss how certain staff officers in 1941 failed to ensure messages were received (Kimmel not receiving the bomb plot message and Short receiving Marshall's war warning after the attack was over). Ask students if we are better at this today, or is it assumed that once we hit the "send" button, the action is complete?

Stand 4
American Preparations

Directions: Retrace the route on Russell Avenue back to South Avenue. Turn right on South Avenue and drive approximately 0.6 miles and turn left to enter Hickam Air Force Base through Porter Gate (this gate is usually unmanned and open during normal duty hours). Once through the gate, immediately turn right on Porter Avenue. After .1 mile you will have to go 180 degrees around the water tower and turn onto Julian Avenue. Julian Avenue will turn into Worthington Avenue. Turn right on 1st Street and then turn right on Vickers Avenue. Vickers Avenue will turn to the left where it becomes Fort Kam Road. Take Fort Kam Road and turn right on Harbor Drive. Travel until you see a black seacoast artillery position on the right. Park in the lot behind the battery. This is Battery Hawkins (the Air Force uses the battery for storage).

Orientation: You are standing at Battery Hawkins. Battery Hawkins was named for US Army Brigadier General (BG) Hamilton Smith Hawkins, a West Point graduate (1855) and Commandant of Cadets at West Point (1888-1892). Hawkins took part in the Battle of San Juan Hill (Cuba, 1898), leading the Sixth and Seventh Regiments in the famous charge up the hill. The battery was completed in 1914 and mounted two 3-inch rapid-fire cannons that were meant to cover the minefield guarding the entrance to Pearl Harbor. The entrance to Pearl Harbor is just to your front. Ford Island is to the north.

Description: The Kingdom of Hawaii granted coaling rights to the US Navy in 1887, beginning a long association for the Navy in Hawaii. In 1898 the United States annexed Hawaii, and it became a US territory in 1900. The United States used the Honolulu Harbor until 1912, when Pearl Harbor was opened as a major forward operating base.

As the Navy started using Pearl Harbor as a major base, the US Army began stationing troops in Hawaii to defend the port. The first contingent of troops was small; some infantry with field artillery and engineers were assigned at Schofield Barracks. As the Navy presence grew, the Army's requirement for defensive organization concurrently grew. The Army established a board of officers to determine requirements, and it recommended a significant array of coastal artillery positions for defending Pearl Harbor and other important facilities in Hawaii. By 1915 the Army had established Fort Ruger, Fort Kamehameha, Fort Armstrong, and Fort DeRussey as facilities to house coastal artillery positions. In all the Army constructed 15 batteries, housing 54 guns (14-inch and 12-inch guns, 12-inch mortars, and smaller rapid-fire weapons like the 3-inch guns at Battery Hawkins as shown in figure 56). The Army also set up mine defenses for the Pearl Harbor entrance by constructing mine wharfs, casemates, and warehouses at Fort Armstrong.

The 1920s saw a drastic increase in the Army's presence in Hawaii. In 1921 the Army organized the Hawaiian Division, consisting of two brigades of two infantry regiments, three field artillery regiments, an engineer regiment, a tank company, and assorted support troops. The division consisted of 13,000 men, with a requirement for expansion to 20,000 during wartime. The Hawaiian National Guard was reorganized at this time and allotted two infantry regiments, the 298th and 299th (900 men each in peacetime but would expand to 3,000 each in wartime).

Figure 56. Battery Hawkins, early 1920s.

As the mobile defenses improved, so did the coastal defenses. In 1921 two mobile regiments, the 41st Coast Artillery Regiment (Railway) and the 55th Coast Artillery (Towed), arrived in Hawaii. The 41st moved its weapons (originally 12-inch mortars but later changed to 8-inch guns) around on railcars on the Oahu Railroad and Land Company's lines and provided 360-degree coastal defense for Oahu. The 55th was armed with 155mm mobile guns pulled by Caterpillar tractors. The 14 existing fixed coast defense batteries were organized into the 15th and 16th Coast Artillery Regiments (Harbor Defense) in 1924. With the advent of the airplane as a major weapon, the arrival in 1921 of the 64th Coast Artillery Regiment (Antiaircraft [AA]) and its 28 3-inch AA guns marked a milestone in Hawaii's defense. In 1925, to provide improved command and control, all of the coast artillery regiments were brigaded under the Hawaiian Separate Coast Artillery Brigade.

The next major change for Army ground units came in 1940 when the 251st Coast Artillery Regiment (California National Guard) arrived with 20 mobile 3-inch AA guns to supplement the island's air defense. Additionally, in July 1941 the 97th and 98th Coast Artillery Regiments (AA) were organized on Oahu and armed with 20 3-inch AA guns each. Hawaii now had four AA regiments, so the 53d Coast Artillery Brigade (AA) was organized to provide them with command and control.

By 1941 the coast artillery of Hawaii had grown to eight regiments—four coastal defense and four AA. To improve command and control, the Hawaiian Department added the Hawaiian Seacoast Defense Command as a "brigade" headquarters for the coastal defenses and converted the Hawaiian Separate Coast Artillery Brigade to the Hawaiian Coast Artillery Command, commanded by Major General (MG) Henry T. Burgin.

Also in 1941 the ground force organization changed. The Hawaiian Division was broken up and converted into the 24th and 25th Divisions. Each division had two active duty regiments and a "round out" regiment from the Hawaiian National Guard. With the change in organization came a change in mission. The 24th Infantry Division (-) would defend the northern half of Oahu, and the 25th Infantry Division (-) would defend the southern half of the island, including critical site security (Pearl Harbor oil tanks, Honolulu water and electric plants, etc.). The 298th Infantry Regiment, 25th Infantry Division, was responsible for defending Koko Head, and the 299th Infantry Regiment, 24th Infantry Division, would defend Maui, the Island of Hawaii, Kauai, and Molokai.

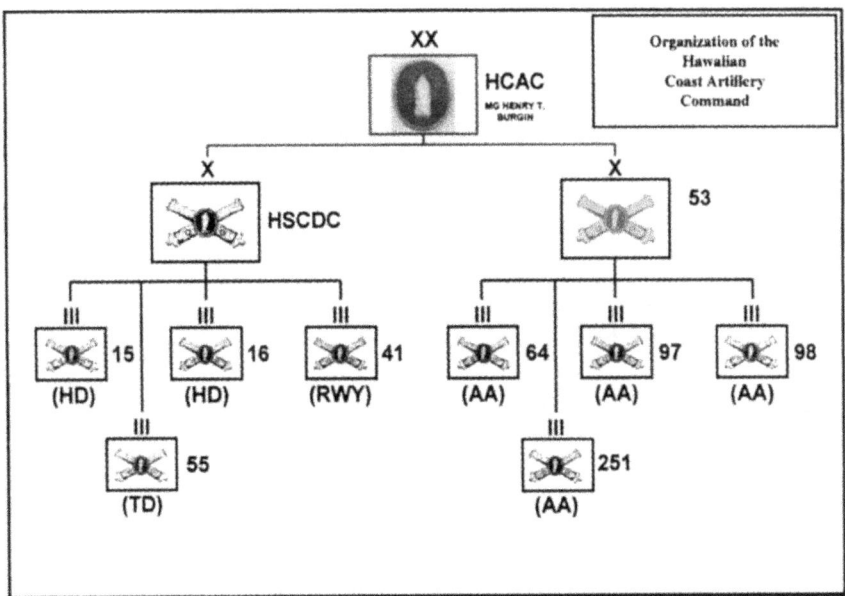

Figure 57.

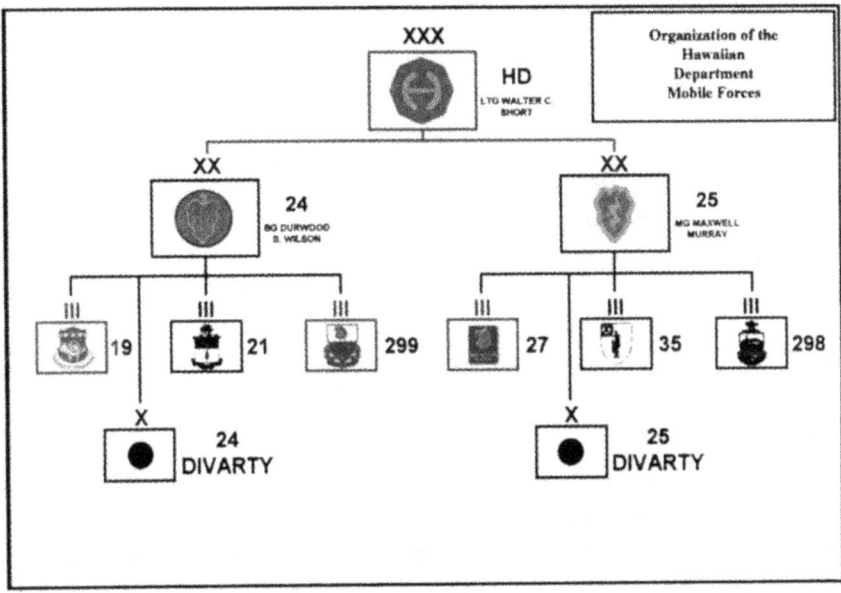

Figure 58.

The Army Air Forces became a member of the military organization of Hawaii in 1917 when the 6th Aero Squadron arrived. For the next 23 years, the air corps expanded as aircraft became more prevalent and as

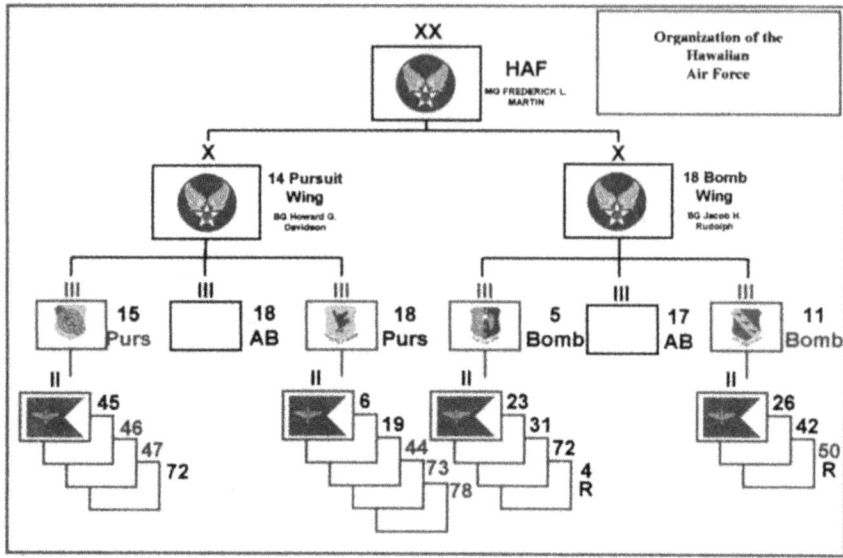

Figure 59.

assets became more available. In August 1919 the 5th Composite Group—consisting of an observation squadron, two pursuit squadrons, and two bombardment squadrons—was organized on Oahu at Wheeler Army Airfield (AAF). In 1927 the air corps increased its pursuit squadrons to five and created the 18th Pursuit Group. In 1931 the 5th and 18th Groups were combined and formed the 18th Composite Wing (which later would be redesignated the 18th Bombardment Wing). In November 1940 the air corps significantly increased its capability by adding the 15th Pursuit Group, 11th Bombardment Group, and 14th Pursuit Wing (composed of the 15th and 18th Pursuit Groups). To provide overall command and control for all air corps elements, the Hawaiian Air Force was organized on 2 November 1940. It consisted of the 14th Pursuit Wing (Wheeler AAF/18th Air Base Group) and the 18th Bombardment Wing (at the newly constructed Hickam AAF/17th Air Base Group).

In December 1941 the US Army had 42,857 men assigned to the Hawaiian Department, commanded by LTG Walter C. Short. The Army's mission was to defend the Pearl Harbor Naval Base (and the fleet berthed there), the City of Honolulu and its harbor, and other installations. The Hawaiian Coast Artillery Command was at or near full strength. The Hawaiian Seacoast Defense Command had more than 100 guns in 33 fixed battery positions, the men were well trained, and ammunition was stored at the batteries. The 53d Coast Artillery Brigade had two regiments at half strength and two at full strength, they were short equipment (they had 86 of

98 3-inch guns, 20 of 120 37mm guns, and 113 of 246 .50-caliber machine guns), and only the 64th Coast Artillery Regiment had ammunition at its battery locations (the assumption was there would be enough notice of an attack to issue ammunition). The two infantry divisions were at about 85 to 90 percent of their authorized strength, but many of the junior enlisted personnel were recent draftees while many of the junior officers were activated reservists who recently arrived from CONUS. The Army Air Forces were near authorized personnel strength and had 152 pursuit aircraft (99 modern P-40s and 53 P-36/26s) and 45 bombers (12 modern B-17s and 33 obsolete B-18s) based at three airfields with a few auxiliary airfields used only for training. Ammunition was not readily available when they were parked at their home fields.

(The staff ride leader may want to move to the edge of the water in front of the battery to discuss naval preparations.)

The Navy had used Pearl Harbor as a forward operating base since 1912, but it did not assign capital ships there until 1939 when the Hawaiian Detachment, consisting of an aircraft carrier, eight cruisers, and 16 destroyers, was based there. The Pacific Fleet was home ported on the west coast (its main base was San Diego) until May 1940, when after completing naval maneuvers, President Roosevelt ordered the Pacific Fleet to remain at Pearl Harbor as a deterrent to Japanese expansion. The facilities at Pearl Harbor were inadequate and required extensive improvement and expansion to service the fleet. Admiral Husband E. Kimmel, Commander, Pacific Fleet, constantly requested reinforcing ships to increase the size and capability of his forward-deployed fleet. Instead, Washington determined that the Atlantic (where the Navy was supporting the convoy effort) was the main effort and ordered Kimmel to send 25 percent of his fleet to the Atlantic—the carrier *Yorktown*; the battleships *Mississippi*, *Idaho*, and *New Mexico*; four cruisers; 17 destroyers; and some auxiliary and supply ships. By December 1941 the Pacific Fleet consisted of three aircraft carriers (one of which was on the west coast undergoing overhaul), nine battleships (one of which was on the west coast undergoing overhaul), 22 cruisers, 53 destroyers, 69 submarines, and 78 PBY aircraft.

The Pacific Fleet's mission was to conduct decisive naval combat operations against an enemy fleet, and as such, it spent most its time at sea training for this mission. In port, ships only took basic self-security measures because naval responsibility for defense fell on the 14th Naval District (Task Force 4), commanded by Rear Admiral Claude C. Bloch. Bloch had a difficult mission because he had no major assets assigned to him for this mission. He had to "borrow" ships to defend the harbor and PBYs for reconnaissance. Any ship defending the harbor was not preparing for war, and the PBYs were the fleet's long-range aerial reconnaissance asset that had few flying hours available for harbor security. In December 1941 the Pacific Fleet was a well-manned, well-trained naval force prepared for maritime combat. When in port the ships were not immediately prepared to engage in combat.

The US Marine Corps had a small complement of troops and equipment on Oahu. Ewa Field was home to Marine Air Group 21, consisting of VMB-232, VMJ-252, VMF-211 (Rear Echelon), and VMB-231 (Rear Echelon). The marines had 10 fighters, 29 bombers, and eight other aircraft at Ewa on 7 December. A complement of 652 marines were assigned at Pearl Harbor in the 1st Defense Battalion (-), 2d Engineer Battalion, 3d Defense Battalion, and 4th Defense Battalion. These marines had four 5-inch AA guns, eight 3-inch AA guns, 20 .50-caliber machine guns, and 16 .30-caliber machine guns. Additionally, 16 ships—eight battleships, two heavy cruisers, four light cruisers and two auxiliaries—had Marine Corps detachments embarked. In December 1941 the marine ground elements were well trained and prepared for combat with ammunition readily available. The Marine Corps aircraft had well-trained pilots but did not have ammunition readily available for the planes.

Vignette: Both Kimmel and Short were concerned about having enough assets to defend Pearl Harbor. In May 1941 Kimmel wrote the CNO:

> The defense of the Fleet base at Pearl Harbor is a matter of considerable concern. We should continue to bring pressure to bear on the Army to get more antiaircraft guns, airplanes, and RADAR equipment to Hawaii and to insure [sic] priority for this over Continental and expanding Army needs.
>
> The naval forces available to Commandant are meager to the point of nonexistence. A Fleet base is a place of rest, recreation, and resustinance and must afford protection of the Fleet at anchor and during entrance and egress independent of the units of the Fleet. If units of a fleet must be employed for its own defense, in its base, its freedom of action for offensive operations is seriously curtailed—possibly to the point where it is tied to the base by the necessities for defense of that base. (*IPHA*, part 22, 364).

Teaching point 1. Combat readiness. Does any US military unit have enough equipment, personnel, training, or money to be completely prepared for war?

The staff ride leader should have the students discuss things that prevent their military units from being 100-percent combat ready. Some of these issues (not a comprehensive list) are training time; personnel shortages; training distracters; training assets, such as fuel, ammunition, and training areas; and equipment shortages. Once you determine that a unit is rarely 100-percent combat ready, lead the group to discuss what units can do to mitigate the dilemma.

Teaching point 2. Preparedness. Most of the units in Hawaii on 7 December 1941 did not have ammunition readily available, believing there would be enough notice to issue ammunition. Does this problem exist today?

The staff ride leader can have the students discuss how really ready their units are today to engage in combat immediately. Did any military unit have the ability to defend on 11 September? Have them talk about where their wartime ammunition is and how long it would take to have their asset (ship, airplane, tank, soldier, marine) ready to respond to a threat. Once this is determined, ask them if in this time of possible surprise terrorist attack this practice is wise. Another possible issue to explore is why we do not have ammunition readily available (safety, ammunition maintenance, accountability).

Stand 5
"Joint" Defenses

Directions: Retrace your route back on Harbor Drive. Turn left on Fort Kam Road. Travel a short distance and turn left on Seaman Avenue. Turn into the dirt parking lot on the left just after the turn. Park and walk to the large battery. This is Battery Hasbrouck.

Orientation: You are standing at Battery Hasbrouck. Battery Hasbrouck was named for BG Henry C. Hasbrouck, West Point class of 1860, who as an artillery officer, served in the Civil War and the Modoc War. The battery was completed in 1914. It housed eight 12-inch M1908 mortars that were housed four to a pit (you can see the steel base rings embedded in the concrete). These breech-loading seacoast mortars could fire a 700-pound projectile 15,200 yards. The entrance to Pearl Harbor is in front of the battery (to the south), and Ford Island is to the north.

Description: General Marshall wrote LTG Short with guidance when Short assumed command of the Hawaiian Department: "The fullest protection of the Fleet is *the* rather than *a* major consideration for us, there can be little question about that. . . . Please keep in mind in all of your negotiations that our mission is to protect the base and the Naval concentrations, and that purpose should be made clearly apparent to Admiral Kimmel." Marshall had clearly communicated Short's mission and Short understood. It is important to remember that the first common link in the chain of command between Kimmel and Short was President Roosevelt. Kimmel

Figure 60. Battery Hasbrouck, early 1920s.

and Short would have to work out any joint plan as a "gentleman's agreement."

Twelve days after assuming command, Short wrote to Marshall to explain his first impressions of the Hawaiian Department. He described his meetings with Kimmel and Bloch and provided a positive impression about the ability to work jointly. Short went on to detail his eight priorities for Hawaii's defense; cooperation with the Navy was number one on the list. Short understood his mission and was working to improve Army-Navy cooperation and the defense of Hawaii.

Air Corps Commander MG Frederick L. Martin and Commander, Patrol Wing 2 (Task Force 9, etc.) Rear Admiral Patrick Bellinger developed the first joint agreement between the Navy and Army. Published on 31 March 1941, the Martin-Bellinger Report, as it has come to be known, described their estimate of the Japanese threat to Hawaii. Prophetically, they wrote in the Possible Enemy Action paragraph:

(a) A declaration of war might be preceeded by:

1. A surprise submarine attack on ships in the operating area.
2. A surprise attack on Oahu including ships and installations in Pearl Harbor.
3. A combination of these two.

(b) It appears that the most likely and dangerous form of attack on Oahu would be an air attack. It is believed that at present such an attack would most likely be launched from one or more carriers which would probably approach inside of three hundred mile.

* * * * *

(e) In a dawn air attack there is a high probability that it could be delivered as a complete surprise in spite of any patrols we might be using and that it might find us in a condition of readiness under which pursuit would be slow to start.

To prevent the Japanese surprise attack that they described, Martin and Bellinger, cognizant of the shortage of long-range reconnaissance aircraft, described the action open to them: "Run daily patrols as far as possible to seaward through 360 degrees to reduce the probabilities of surface or air surprise. This would be desirable but can only be effectively maintained with present personnel and material for a very short period and as a practicable measure cannot, therefore, be undertaken unless other intelligence indicates that a surface raid is probable within rather narrow time limits."

The report went on to detail how the two branches would locate and attack any fleet (using both Navy and Army long-range aircraft under Navy control) and defend against any air attack using all fighters on the island—Army, Navy, and Marine Corps under Army control. Additionally, the aviators detailed an aircraft readiness system that identified percentages of aircraft prepared for combat and a time limit for launching the aircraft.

On 11 April 1941 Short and Bloch (acting for Kimmel) published the most comprehensive joint plan for defending Hawaii, the Joint Coastal Frontier Defense Plan (JCFDP). This gentleman's agreement between the Army and Navy detailed the delimitation of areas, established a Joint Planning Committee to continue joint planning, listed tasks for each service, required each service to write supporting defensive plans, and obligated further agreements on allocating supplies and services. The plan's joint task was "to hold Oahu as a main outlying naval base, and to control and protect shipping in the Coastal Zone." The Army was tasked "to hold Oahu against attacks by sea, land, and air forces and against hostile sympathizers; to support the naval forces." The Army had 16 requirements to accomplish the task (defending Oahu, bomber support for naval aircraft in major offensive sea operations, etc.), including establishing an Aircraft Warning Service (AWS).

In the plan the Navy was tasked "to patrol the Coastal Zone and to control and protect shipping therein; to support Army forces." The 16 requirements spelled out how the Navy would accomplish its task; the most important was "distant reconnaissance." The Army had only 12 aircraft capable of conducting long-distance patrols, and the Navy had 72 PBYs, so the Navy assumed responsibility for distant reconnaissance.

The two services now had good joint plans for defending Pearl Harbor and the other critical installations in Hawaii. They delineated responsibilities, attempted to overcome shortages and weaknesses of the other service, and tried to use the particular strengths of each service. However, the plans had two flaws—their success depended on advance notice and good intelligence.

In October and November 1941 the Navy and Army discussed establishing a joint headquarters for both commanders, but Kimmel thought the disadvantages outweighed the advantages and decided not to collocate. However, the services did create the Joint Harbor Control Post, which had elements from the Coast Artillery, Air Corps, Fleet Air Arm, Submarine

Force, and the Naval District to command and control the water around the port. The commanders thought this facility could accomplish the same thing as a joint headquarters.

Part of the JCFDP called for the Army to establish the AWS, a service consisting of radar stations, observation posts, and an air-warning center for command and control. By December 1941 the Army had six SCR-270 mobile radar stations and three SCR-271 fixed radar sites. Locations had been found and coordinated for the six mobile locations, and they were operational in December 1941. The three fixed sets lacked some equipment, and no terrain was coordinated for their emplacement. Some of the locations selected were on US Park Service property, and the War Department was having difficulty getting Interior Department permission to emplace the radars on their property because they would be an eyesore.

The radar sets were under the Army Signal Corps' control, much to the chagrin of the Air Corps, which thought the radars should be under its control. The radar operators had gone to sea with Navy ships equipped with radar to learn how the radar worked and to train on the systems, which were similar to the ground stations. All of the radars and observation posts were connected by telephone to the Air Warning Center at Fort Shafter. There plotters marked the flight paths of located targets so the center's director, with assistance from Navy and Air Corps liaisons, could determine

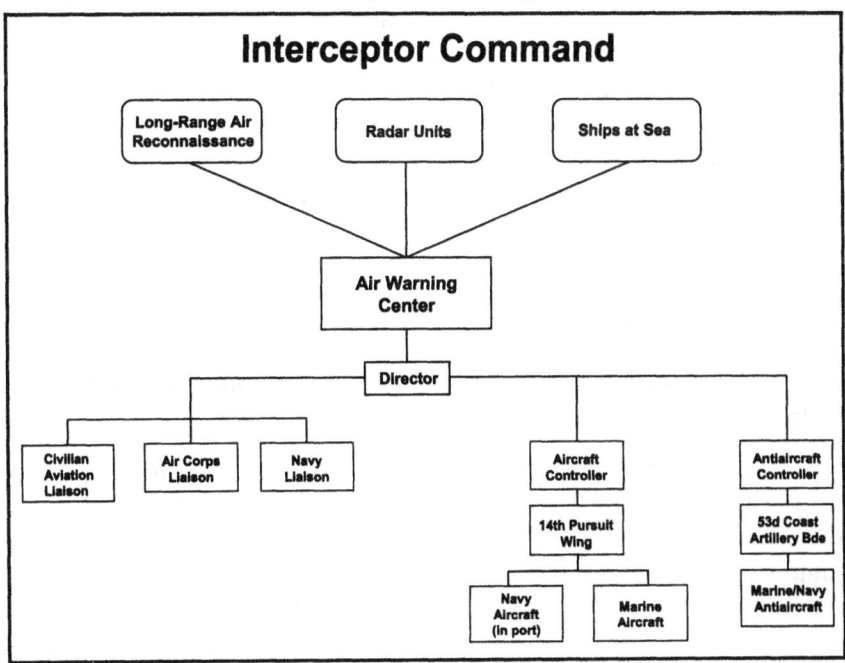

Figure 61.

if the planes were friendly or an enemy. If the planes were enemy or undetermined, the director could ask the pursuit liaison to launch aircraft.

To maximize the radar's potential, the Hawaiian Department decided to create the Interceptor Command based on a model the British were using. BG Howard C. Davidson, Commander, 14th Pursuit Wing, would command the Interceptor Command. The command would consist of AWS (under Air Corps control), the 14th Pursuit Wing, the 53d Coast Artillery Brigade (AA) (with control of Marine Corps AA), and a liaison section from the Navy to control Navy and Marine Corps fighters. The key for the Interceptor Command was the Air Warning Center at Fort Shafter, where aircraft were tracked and determined to be an enemy or a friend. If determined to be an enemy, the director could launch fighters (Army, Navy, or Marine Corps) and coordinate AA protection. During a joint exercise on 12 November 1941, US Navy aircraft launched from a carrier 80 miles from Oahu were seen by the radars, and within 6 minutes, fighters were launched and intercepted the "aggressors" 30 miles from Oahu. The Army and Navy now had tested a reliable system for defending Oahu from the air and planned to activate the Interceptor Command in late December 1941.

Vignette: Shortly after assuming command, Short wrote of his impressions of the Navy commanders and his thoughts on jointness: "Since assuming command, I have had two conferences with Admiral Kimmel and two with Admiral Bloch. I have found them both most approachable and cooperative in every way. I have told them that from my point of view there will be no hair splitting, but that the one thing that would affect any decision where there is an apparent conflict between the Army and the Navy in the use of facilities would be the question of what could produce the greatest combined effort of the two forces. They have assured me that they will take exactly the same view. From my brief intercourse with them I feel that our relations should be extremely cordial." (*IPHA*, part 24, 1,835.)

Teaching point 1. Joint command. Did Kimmel and Short have an effective joint command?

The staff ride leader should have the students discuss the joint command structure's effectiveness and weaknesses. Items to consider during the discussion include the command arrangement (there was no formal joint command and no joint doctrine), colocating the commanders (Did the two have to be together, or could they communicate via phone?), and delineating tasks. (All like task units such as bombers, fighters, and AA units worked for a single commander.) Once the students have discussed this, ask them if today, with factors like Goldwater-Nichols, we are better at being joint. Items to consider here include sharing assets (How much do the marines like to "share" their aircraft with the air component commander and the Army like to "share" Patriot missiles?), communications (How well do the individual service's communications interface with the others?), cultural difference, and doctrinal differences.

Teaching point 2. Dependence on early warning. Were the joint plans too dependent on having enough early warning?

The staff ride leader can have the students discuss how dependent the JCFDP (of which the Martin-Bellinger Report became an annex) was on having early warning. It was a good plan, but to be effective, the United States had to conduct reconnaissance in a 360-degree fan around the island. Due to assets, this was impractical. When the discussion on the JCFDP wanes, ask the students if today's planners are too dependent on having "enough notice." Ask them if the assumptions in today's plans allow for a "buildup" phase or time to get ready (condition setting). Ask the students if transformation (units of action, composite wings, etc.) is the answer.

Stand 6
Preparedness and Early Warning

Directions: Drive back up Seaman Avenue and turn left on Fort Kam Road. After a short distance, pull into the parking lot on the left (you can see Pearl Harbor inlet from the road). Park and walk to the water.

Orientation: Standing at the entrance to Pearl Harbor. Every ship entering or departing the harbor has to pass through here. Pearl Harbor anchorage is to the north. Fort Kamehameha is to the southeast.

Description: The Army and Navy each had a system of alerts that numbered 1 through 3. Unfortunately, the Army's system had 1 as the most minor alert, and 3 was full alert. The Navy did the opposite; 3 was the minor alert, and 1 was full alert. This difference was not known to either service and would lead to problems later in the year.

Throughout 1941 the US forces in Hawaii spent their time training and standing alerts to defend the island, based on warnings from Washington. Various levels of joint exercises were conducted on 26 February, 3-5 March, 24 March, 19 May, 12-24 May, 13 October, 27 October, 10 November, and 12 November. All through the year, alerts were called that required the services to exhibit different levels of preparedness and curtailed training. The first alert of the year was on 3 March, and the next was conducted 25-30 July.

On 26 November the Japanese government rejected a US proposal that would have calmed the situation between the two nations. Washington decided that war was closer than ever and on 27 November sent warnings out to all subordinate commanders around the world. Kimmel received his message that started with, "This dispatch is to be considered a war warning." The message went on to detail how negotiations had broken down and that Japan would strike somewhere within the next few days (the Philippines, Thai Peninsula, Kra Peninsula, and Borneo were mentioned in the message). It ordered the naval commanders to "Execute an appropriate defensive deployment preparatory to carrying out tasks assigned in [Navy war plans]." Kimmel pondered the message but assumed the message meant the Japanese would attack somewhere other than Pearl Harbor. To continue his training regimen, his only action was to authorize the depth charging of any submerged submarine detected around Oahu.

Short also received a warning from the War Department informing him that negotiations with Japan had terminated and that hostile action could occur at any moment. He was told that the United States desired Japan to make the first overt act but that this should not restrict his defensive preparations. He was told to take measures to prepare, but not to alarm, the civilian populace and to report the actions he had taken. The Navy had told Short that the Japanese carriers were in home waters, and he knew that Japan did not have aircraft with sufficient range to reach Hawaii from any of the Mandate Islands, so he determined that sabotage was his greatest danger. He therefore ordered alert 1, which called for protection against sabotage. Each coastal battery, AA position, and key facility was guarded 24 hours a day, and aircraft were lined up wingtip to wingtip for easier guarding. If Short had selected alert 2 or 3, he would have had to issue ammunition to all of his positions, and he was sure this action would alarm the civilian population, a direct violation of his orders.

Once he decided on alert 1, Short sent a message to the War Department, "RURD [Reference your radiogram] 472 report department alerted to prevent sabotage liaison with Navy." The next day, 28 November, Short received a reply from Army Adjutant General MG Emory S. Adams: "critical situation demands that all precautions be taken immediately against subversive activities . . . initiate forthwith all additional measures necessary to provide protection of your establishments, property, and equipment against sabotage." As a precaution, Short also ordered the AWS to be in full operation from 0400-0700 everyday. (It was also in operation from 0700-1100 and 1200-1600 Monday through Friday for training.) Short informed Kimmel that he had gone to alert 1, but Kimmel thought alert 1 was the highest alert.

After Kimmel gave his antisubmarine instructions, reports of suspected submarines were so numerous that the sightings became routine. Additionally, a few ships even dropped depth charges on suspected sightings. From 27 November until 7 December the Navy inshore patrol maintained vigilance while the Army defended against saboteurs.

Early on the morning of 7 December, five Japanese fleet submarines launched the midget submarines they had carried from Japan. Concurrently, minesweepers *Condor* and *Crossbill* were sweeping the entrance of Pearl Harbor for any mines (Japanese submarines were able to plant mines). At 0342 *Condor's* crewmembers spotted a periscope in the restricted area just outside the entrance to Pearl Harbor and blinked a message to the USS *Ward*, the destroyer on inshore patrol. Lieutenant William W. Outerbridge had just assumed command of the *Ward* two days prior, but he did not hesitate to take his ship to general quarters and hunt for the submarine. Outerbridge searched for the submarine for the next 38 minutes but gave up and secured from general quarters at 0453.

At 0630 the USS *Antares*, a supply ship, was entering Pearl Harbor with a lighter in tow when its captain noticed a conning tower of a semi-submerged submarine following them. *Ward* was again notified and went to general quarters at 0640. Outerbridge maneuvered his old four-stack destroyer within 50 meters of the submarine and opened fire with 4-inch guns. The second shot hit the submarine where the conning tower joined the hull of the submarine. *Ward* immediately dropped a full pattern of depth charges on the sinking submarine. A PBY on patrol also dropped depth charges on the target. Outerbridge immediately reported to the Naval District watch officer: "We have attacked, fired upon, and dropped depth charges upon submarine operating in defensive sea area." The report worked its way up the chain until it reached Kimmel, who also received a report from Patrol Wing 2, reporting their attack on the submarine. Kimmel was not certain this was a real attack because of all the reports of submarines earlier in the week, but he ordered the ready-duty destroyer to the area. The Navy never informed the Army of the sighting.

Figure 62. USS *Ward*.

The AWS had gone into operation at 0400, 7 December and was scheduled to shut down at 0700. At the Opana Radar Station, Private Joseph Lockard had been instructing Private George Elliot on operating the radar. When the two learned that their transportation would be late, Lockard decided to keep the station operating to continue training. At 0702 Elliot observed a large formation of airplanes approaching Oahu from the north (the first Japanese attack wave), which puzzled the two soldiers as they discussed what to do.

Finally, Lockard and Elliot decided to call the Air Warning Center at Fort Shafter. The operator at the center told Elliot that everyone had already departed but then noticed Lieutenant Kermit Tyler, the pursuit

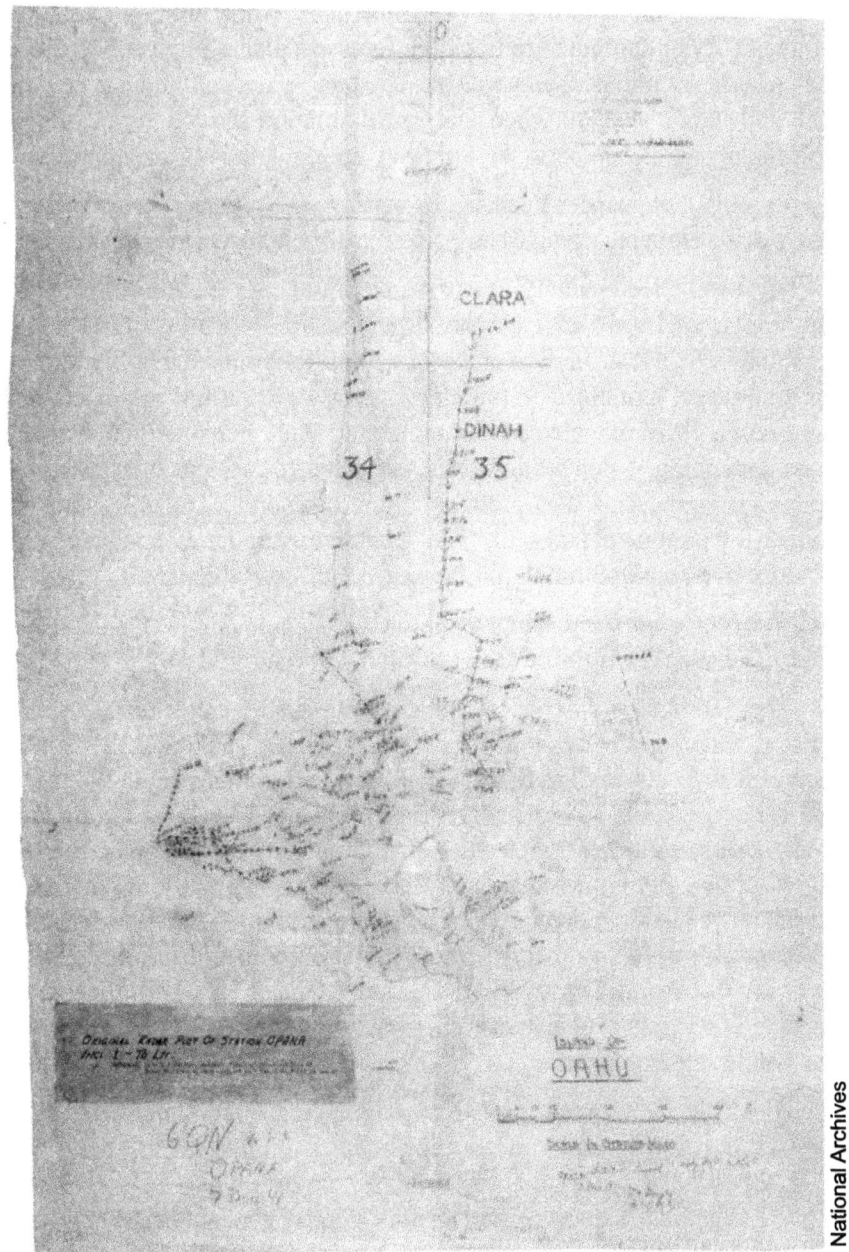

Figure 63. Radar track from Opana Radar Site, 7 December 1941.

officer who had been on duty that morning. Elliot explained that his station was tracking the biggest sighting they had ever seen and gave Tyler all of the pertinent information. A friend had told Tyler that a flight of 12 B-17 bombers was scheduled to arrive from the north that morning (Opana was

97

in fact tracking them, too), so he told Elliot not to worry about the sighting. Elliot and Tyler continued to track the Japanese planes approaching Oahu for the next 19 minutes, and with the Japanese planes 20 miles away, the men shut down at 0739 when their transportation arrived. Tyler did not inform anyone of the report, so the Navy did not know of the sighting.

At 0740 Commander Fuchida, the Japanese air commander, ordered his planes that were approaching Oahu "undetected" to form into attack formations.

Vignette: Lieutenant Tyler was on duty at the Air Warning Center for only the second time on 7 December and was only there as the center's pursuit officer, not as director or aircraft controller. While being questioned for the Roberts Commission (an investigative commission convened after the attack), Tyler reflected on the moment: "Well, perhaps I should have done something. I don't know, but it seemed to me that there was still nothing irregular, that they probably might be friendly craft. So I thought about it for a moment and said, 'Well don't worry about it,' and went back awaiting the hour and time until the next relief." *(IPHA,* part 22, 221.)

Teaching point. Reporting. With two very significant events occurring before the attack, why were the Army and Navy surprised?

There are many approaches the staff ride leader can use for this discussion. One approach is to discuss "crying wolf." Ask the students how natural it is to not say anything because you are afraid people will think you are crying wolf. Ask the students how you can prepare and train your soldiers/sailors/airmen/marines to report anything that they think is suspicious. Are we better at this today? Read the students the following transcript between the Federal Aviation Administration (FAA) headquarters (HQ) and one of its command centers (CC) on 11 September 2001 at 0949. They are discussing United Flight 93 that ultimately crashed in Pennsylvania at 1003 (this is after two planes had hit the World Trade Center and one had hit the Pentagon):

FAA HQ: They're pulling Jeff away to go talk about United 93.
CC: Uh, do we want to think, uh, about scrambling aircraft?
FAA HQ: Oh, God, I don't know.
CC: Uh, that's a decision somebody's gonna have to make probably in the next 10 minutes.
FAA HQ: Uh, ya know everybody just left the room.

Another approach is talking about information sharing. Query the students: "The Navy had one piece of information and the Army had another. If one commander had both pieces of information, would he have been better prepared for the attack?"

Stand 7
Japanese Air Superiority

Directions: Leave the parking lot and turn left on Fort Kam Road. When the road bends to the right, it becomes Vickers Avenue. Take Vickers Avenue for approximately 0.8 mile until you see a large white building—Pacific Air Force (PACAF) HQ—on the right. Parking is difficult at this location. First, attempt to park in the parking lot before reaching the building (west of the building). You may have to drive past it, turn left onto Atterbury Circle, and park by the 15th Air Base Wing HQ. Once you are parked, walk to PACAF HQ and conduct the stand in the grass by the building (there are numerous locations on the building where damage from 7 December is still visible).

Orientation: We are now going to transition to the attack on Pearl Harbor itself. It is important that we look at the results of when we fail. This building is home to the PACAF HQ. In December 1941 it was the Hale Makai ("House by the Sea" in Hawaiian) Barracks. Completed on 30 September 1941 (but troops had been occupying parts of it since January 1940), the barracks housed 3,200 soldiers and was the largest barracks in the Army. Besides housing 3,200 soldiers, it had a large mess hall in the center that the troop wings all connected to, two barbershops, a dispensary, a tailor shop, a laundry, and a PX shoppette.

Description: At 0530, 7 December 1941 the Japanese 1st Air Fleet was 230 miles north of Oahu when the cruisers *Tone* and *Chickuma* launched seaplanes for reconnaissance missions. One airplane was tasked to observe Pearl Harbor while the other was to see if there were any ships in the Lahaina Bay anchorage, which the Pacific Fleet sometimes used. The aircraft over Lahaina Bay reported it was empty; the Pearl Harbor aircraft reported nine battleships, a heavy cruiser, and six light cruisers in the harbor. Its pilot also provided a weather report of the area (the winds were 14 meters from the east, and the ceiling was 1,700 meters with 70-percent cover).

At 0600 the Japanese started launching their first-wave airplanes, of which 183 of the planned 189 successfully launched. Japanese Air Commander Fuchida formed his aircraft with the high-level bombers leading at 9,800 feet, the dive bombers to their left at 11,000 feet, the torpedo bombers to the right at 9,200 feet, and the fighters dispersed throughout. As soon as the first wave was gone, the Japanese fleet continued sailing to the south while the second-wave aircraft were brought up from the hangar decks to prepare for launch. At 0715 167 of the planned 171 planes for the second

Figure 64. Japanese planes prepare for takeoff, 7 December 1941.

wave took off for Oahu. A total of 350 Japanese planes would attack US ships and facilities.

The Japanese had many contingency plans for the attack, including plans for complete surprise and plans if they were detected. If they achieved surprise, the slow and vulnerable torpedo planes would lead the attack, but if surprise was lost, the dive bombers would lead so the American AA gunners would be firing high into the sky when the torpedo planes approached. At 0740 Fuchida determined that the Japanese had achieved complete surprise and fired a single signal flare to indicate that. All of the planes moved into position except one group of fighters. Fuchida assumed that group had not seen the flare, so he fired another one. Seeing the second flare, the dive bombers assumed that the Japanese had not achieved surprise and they were to lead the attack. The torpedo planes did not see the second flare and still assumed that they would lead the attack. After months of planning, the plan was unraveling because of a simple signal error.

The 40 torpedo bombers with fighter escort broke off from the formation north of Oahu to fly down the western side of the Waianae Range, where they divided into two groups. One group would attack from the northeast, and one would attack from the southeast. Twenty-five dive bombers with fighters departed the formation to attack Wheeler AAF from two directions. Twenty-six dive bombers with fighter escort would attack Hickam AAF and Pearl Harbor NAS. With Fuchida in the lead, the 49

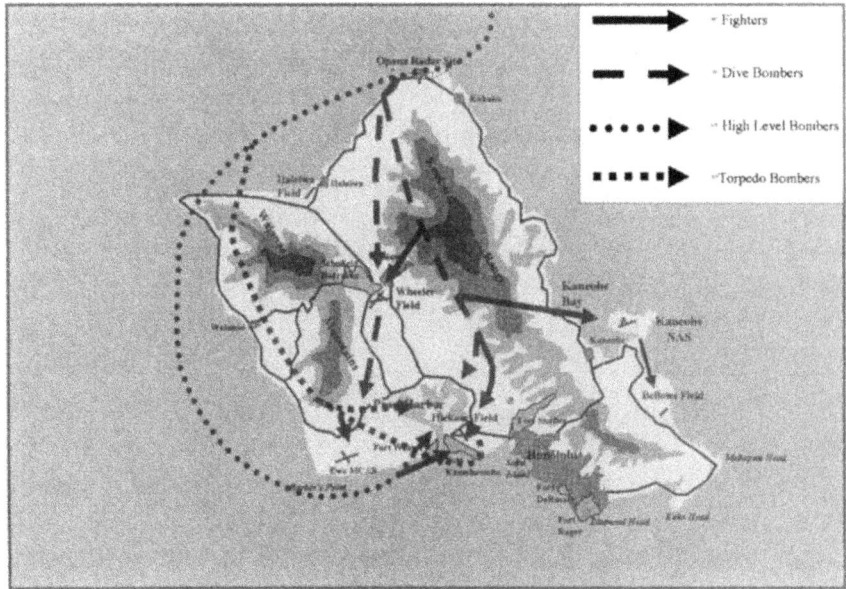

Figure 65. First-wave plan.

high-level bombers flew around the west side of Oahu and planned to approach Pearl Harbor from the southwest.

At 0750, 25 "Val" dive bombers and seven Zero fighters arrived over Wheeler AAF and started their attack. In response to alert 1, all Army fighters in Hawaii were lined up on the tarmac parked wing to wing. The Vals dropped their bombs and made a few strafing passes, and the Zeros also strafed once they were sure there were not fighters in the air. Some of the dive bombers, once they had dropped their bombs, proceeded to Ewa Field to strafe the Marine Corps aircraft there.

At 0752, shortly after the attack commenced on Wheeler, the Japanese struck the PBYs of Patrol Wing 2 at Kaneohe. Nine Zero fighters made numerous strafing passes at the large floating planes, some ashore and some tied to their berths in the water. In just 8 minutes, many of Kaneohe's aircraft were burning, and the sailors tried to save as many as they could. One of the Zeros departed Kaneohe and strafed Bellows Field, a small auxiliary field, causing minor damage.

Nineteen fighters accompanied the torpedo bombers, and when they arrived over Ewa at 0753, they did not see any American planes in the air, so they broke off to strafe the marine aircraft parked wing to wing. Nine Val dive bombers attacked the 35 PBYs at Pearl Harbor NAS on Ford Island at 0755. The Japanese pilots dropped their bombs on the parked aircraft and the hangars at the southern end of the island, destroying or

Figure 66. Wheeler AAF under attack, 7 December.

badly damaging 26 aircraft in short time.

The aircraft of the 18th Bombardment Wing at Hickam were, for the most part, parked wing to wing when the Japanese arrived at 0800. Seventeen Val dive bombers and eight Zero fighters attacked the vulnerable aircraft, the hangars, and the barracks, killing 25 men in the barracks mess hall. Hickam was in flames when the Japanese planes departed. In short time the Japanese had crippled the American air capability and ensured that enemy aircraft would not hinder the planes tasked to attack Pearl Harbor.

Vignette: The Japanese caught the Americans "flat-footed" on the morning of 7 December. There are many accounts of service members being initially shocked by the attack but quickly overcoming it to do their duty. MG Frederick L. Martin, Commander, Hawaiian Air Force remembered his reaction to the attack: "This was about—this bombing was occurring probably less than a mile from my position. I saw the red circle on the wing tip of this airplane as it pulled out, and I knew it was Japanese. I rushed back to the telephone, called General Davidson, who was in charge of the intercept command, to tell him to get his pursuit ships in the air just as fast as he could, and he said they were being attacked at the same time and that they were struggling to get their ships in position so they could get them off." (*IPHA*, part 22, 194.)

Teaching point. Air superiority. Ninety-four of 183 planes of the first wave were dedicated to the air superiority role. Did the Japanese dedicate too many assets to this mission?

Air superiority always makes for a good discussion, and the staff ride leader can take full advantage of this while leading the discussion by being the "devil's advocate." If students say the air superiority mission was key, remind them that the extensive fuel tank farm on Pearl Harbor was never attacked and ask if 51 dive bombers could have caused that key installation any damage. If they say the Japanese dedicated too many assets to air superiority, remind them that only 14 American planes got into the air that day, but they shot down 11 Japanese planes. Once this discussion fades, ask them if air superiority is the most important operation today. Compare and contrast using aircraft in support of ground forces versus using the planes to gain and maintain air superiority. Again, being the devil's advocate will work for this part of the discussion.

Stand 8
Japanese Torpedo Attack

Directions: Travel west on Boquet Boulevard. Turn right on Moore Street and immediately turn right on Julian Avenue. Go 180 degrees around the water tower and go northeast on Porter Avenue. Enter Pearl Harbor through the Porter Avenue gate and turn right on South Avenue. After 1 mile, at the stop sign, bear to the left on North Street. After 0.4 mile, turn right on Makalapa Road and exit Pearl Harbor. Turn left on State Route 99 (Kamehameha Highway), drive 1.2 miles, and turn left to enter Ford Island on Ford Island Boulevard. You will have to stop at the security gate (just like when you entered Pearl Harbor the first time). From the security checkpoint, drive 1.1 miles and turn right on Saratoga Boulevard. Drive 0.5 mile and park in the lot by the water. Dismount and move to the monument with the flagpole.

Orientation: Standing at the USS *Utah* memorial. On 7 December the USS *Utah* was berthed here, a space often occupied by aircraft carriers. The USS *Utah* was a Florida-class battleship commissioned in 1911 that saw service at Vera Cruz, Mexico in 1914 and in the Atlantic during World War I. Due to the limits of the Washington Naval Treaty, it was converted to a radio-controlled target ship in 1931. The Navy also used the *Utah* as an AA training ship by adding the requisite guns/machine guns and instructors.

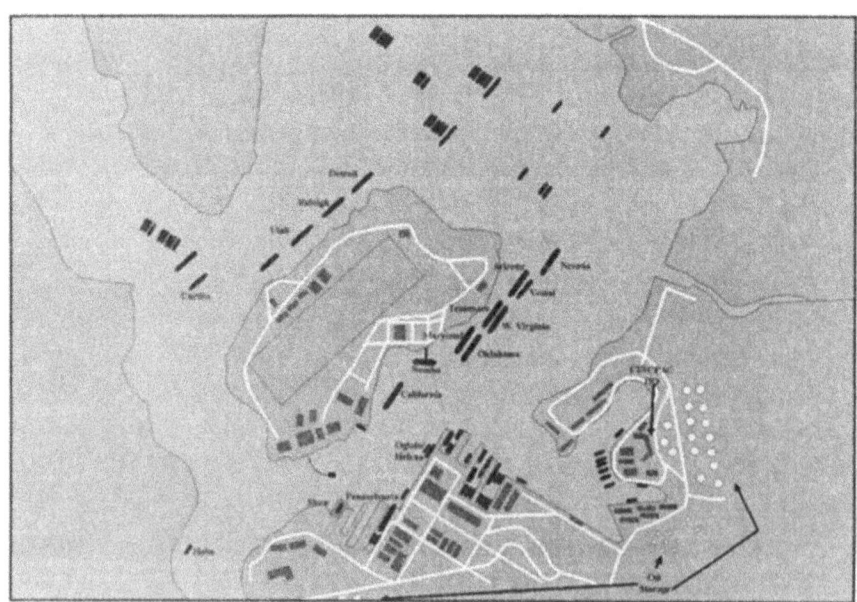

Figure 67. Pearl Harbor at 0757, 7 December 1941.

Figure 68. Torpedo attack on Pearl Harbor. A geyser rises from the USS *West Virginia* after it has been hit by a torpedo. The USS *Utah* and USS *Raleigh* have also been hit.

On 7 December the *Utah* was moored here at berth F-11. The USS *Raleigh*, a light cruiser, was moored in front of it, and the USS *Tangier*, a seaplane tender, was moored aft of it. Across Ford Island to the east was Battleship Row where all of the battleships moored.

Description: At 0757, 7 December 1941 the Japanese began their attack on the ships in the harbor. Sixteen "Kate" torpedo planes approached the west side of Ford Island where aircraft carriers usually moored when in port. Despite warning not to waste their torpedoes on small or noncombatant ships, two planes' torpedoes slammed into the USS *Utah*, and one torpedo hit the USS *Raleigh*. In 13 short minutes, the *Utah* capsized, trapping 58 sailors who are still entombed to this day. The USS *Raleigh* started to list heavily and was in great danger of rolling over, but Herculean efforts by the crew and other sailors saved it from overturning. Some of the Japanese torpedo pilots attacking from the west realized these were poor targets and flew over Ford Island to attack ships on the other side. One torpedo the Japanese dropped passed under the minelayer USS *Oglala* and hit the USS *Helena*, a light cruiser. The concussion from the explosion on the *Helena* holed the *Oglala*, and it capsized at 1000.

While the attack was going on to the west, 24 Kate torpedo bombers approached Battleship Row from the east. Using Southeast Loch as a guide (described by someone as a "bowling alley leading right to Battleship Row"), the planes approached Battleship Row where the USS *Oklahoma* and USS *West Virginia* were centered in their windshields. Within 5 minutes, five torpedoes had opened the port side of the *Oklahoma*, and it began to roll over. Soon, "Abandon ship!" was ordered, and the sailors tried to escape as the *Oklahoma* continued to roll over, only stopping when its superstructure stuck in the mud. The *Oklahoma* lost 429 men that day. Seven torpedoes in rapid succession hit the *West Virginia*, and only the counterflooding the captain ordered saved it from the same fate as the *Oklahoma*. It settled to the bottom with the deck barely awash with 106 of the crew killed, including the captain, Mervyn Bennion, who earned the Medal of Honor. Subsequent torpedo pilots sought other targets to hit, and two torpedoes hit the USS *California*. Prepared for an inspection the next day, all of its hatches were open, so the ship quickly flooded and eventually sank with her deck awash, 98 of the crew perishing. One of the last planes slammed a torpedo into the USS *Nevada*, causing damage but not a fatal blow.

Forty torpedo planes attacked that morning and hit with 19 torpedoes—48-percent hit rate—sinking battleships *Oklahoma*, *West Virginia*, and *California*. Torpedoes sank the target ship *Utah* and minelayer *Oglala*, and the cruisers *Raleigh* and *Helena* were badly damaged. Five of the 40 torpedo planes were shot down and 10 were damaged.

Vignette: Commander Jesse Kenworthy, Jr. was the executive officer of the USS *Oklahoma* and the senior officer aboard (the captain was ashore on authorized pass). In his official report, he recalled how quickly his ship was doomed:

> As I attempted to get to the Conning tower over the decks slippery with oil and water, I felt the shock of another very heavy explosion on the port side. By this time the ship was listing from 25 to 35 degrees and was continuing to list further. It was now obvious that the ship was going to continue to roll over and I climbed over the boat deck toward the starboard side. Men were beginning to come up from below through hatches and gun ports and from them it was learned that the ship was filling with water in many spaces below. As I reached the starboard side, I met Lieutenant Commander Hobby, the First Lieutenant, and with him concluded that the ship was fast becoming untenable and that an effort should be made to save as many men as possible. The word was passed for all hands

to abandon ship, and the men were directed to leave over the starboard side and to walk and climb over the ship's side and onto the bottom as it rolled over. At about this time another heavy explosion was felt on the port side and the ship began to roll over rapidly. The men went over the starboard side, climbing over the side and bottom and many went into the water to swim to the *Maryland*. (Enclosure E to CINCPAC action report, Serial 0479, 15 February 1942, World War II Action Reports, Modern Military Branch, National Archives and Records Administration, College Park, MD.)

Teaching point. Persistence. Why was the Japanese torpedo attack so incredibly successful?

The staff ride leader can let the students discuss this as they see fit, but one area should be emphasized. Fuchida knew there was a problem with using torpedoes at Pearl Harbor, but he solved the problem from the bottom up by gathering the best torpedo plane crews and giving them the latitude to solve the problem the way they saw fit. Let the students discuss this, and ask them how the US military solves difficult problems today. Ask them if it solves problems from the bottom up or from the top down.

Stand 9
Japanese High-Level Attack

Directions: Retrace your route back on Saratoga Boulevard. At the traffic circle, go 180 degrees around and continue on Saratoga Boulevard to the yield sign. Continue straight and park in the parking lot. Dismount the vehicle and walk to the water.

Orientation: The mooring pylon to the front is where the USS *Tennessee* was tied up on 7 December. The USS *Arizona* Memorial rests over the middle of the *Arizona*, and the white buoy marks the front of the ship. Southeast Loch is directly to your front. The rest of the battleships were moored to the south.

Description: As the torpedo planes ravaged the Pacific Fleet, Fuchida personally led the high-level bombers from the southwest toward Battleship Row. The high-level bombers were in 10 triangle groups of five planes each (one group only had four planes because one high-level bomber aborted on takeoff), and each group had a battleship as its target. As established during training, the planes were flying at 11,000 feet, and when the experienced lead aircraft dropped its bomb, the entire group released its 1,750-pound bombs. Fuchida had briefed his high-level pilots to go around for a second pass if their target was obscured, and some groups had to make two or more passes. Fuchida led the first group toward his target, the USS *Nevada*, but it was obscured and they went around.

The next three groups and the sixth group dropped their bombs on the *Tennessee* and *West Virginia*. Two bombs hit the *Tennessee*, but the bombs had a low-order detonation. The first bomb hit turret 2 and rendered all three guns inoperable, and the second bomb penetrated turret 3 and damaged one of the guns. Two bombs also hit the sinking *West Virginia* but did not explode. The first bomb pierced turret 3 but did no damage. The second bomb penetrated the deck and was later found on the second deck. The fifth and ninth groups aimed their bombs for the *Arizona*. Two bombs hit the USS *Vestal*, a repair ship tied off next to the *Arizona*. One bomb penetrated three decks and exploded, causing fires and flooding. The second bomb passed completely through the ship without exploding and caused more flooding. Four bombs hit the *Arizona*. One bomb hit turret 4, and two more bombs hit the aft portion of the deck. A fourth bomb hit the deck near turret 2 and passed through two decks before exploding. The explosion punctured an oil tank and caused an intense fire that ignited a small powder magazine (1,000 pounds of propellant used to launch the ship's observation aircraft), causing the 14-inch and 5-inch

Figure 69. Battleship Row as seen from a Japanese high-level bomber.

Figure 70. The USS *Arizona* exploding after being hit by a high-level bomb.

magazines to explode. Ninety-nine tons of powder was in those magazines, and when they exploded they demolished the ship's bow. Along with Rear Admiral Isaac Kidd, commander of Battleship Division One, and Captain Franklin Van Valkenburgh, 1,177 of the *Arizona's* 1,700-man crew were killed.

The seventh, eighth, and Fucida's groups dropped their bombs on the USS *Maryland*, which was hit by two bombs that only had low-level detonations. One of the small explosions however, caused extensive flooding. The last group was tasked to bomb the USS *California*, but smoke from the furiously burning *Arizona* blanketed Battleship Row, and all of the bombs missed their targets. Twelve of 49 bombs from the high-level bombers hit their targets (a 24-percent hit rate), and in six of those hits, the bombs malfunctioned. However, one bomb found a "lucky" spot, destroyed a battleship, and killed more than 1,000 men. None of the high-level bombers was shot down, but eight were damaged.

Vignette: Lieutenant Commander Samuel G. Fuqua, Damage Control Officer of the USS *Arizona*, was the senior surviving crew member. He was awarded the Medal of Honor for his coolness, leadership, and concern for his sailors on 7 December. He remembered 7 December:

Figure 71. Battleship Row after the first wave; the USS *Arizona* is burning, and the USS *Oklahoma* has capsized.

I glanced up. I saw a bomb dropping which appeared to me was going to land on me or close by. The next thing I remember I came to on deck in a position about six feet aft of the starboard gangway. I got to my feet and looked around to see what it was that had knocked me down. Then I saw I was lying about six feet from a bomb hole in the deck. . . . I would judge about 8:15 or 8:20 I saw a tremendous mass of flames, the height of 300 feet, rise in the air forward, and shook the ship aft as if it would fall apart like a pack of cards. . . . Being that the ship was no longer in fighting condition, I ordered the remaining people in the after turrets to abandon ship . . . at about 0845, I made a thorough search of the after part of the ship, which was accessible, for wounded and injured personnel. . . . I finally left the ship myself at 0915, and proceeded to the receiving barracks at Pearl Harbor to report in.

Fuqua returned to the *Arizona* two days later after the fires were out and continued the story: "We found the admiral's body on the boat deck, or we found a body which I believe to be the admiral's body on the boat deck, just at the foot of the flag bridge ladder. The captain's body was never found. However, the captain's ring and some coat buttons were found on the flag bridge." Rear Admiral Kidd and Captain Van Valkenburgh were also awarded the Medal of Honor. (*IPHA*, part 23, 634-36.)

Teaching point. Dealing with disaster. How did Lieutenant Commander Fuqua, after being knocked unconscious by a bomb and seeing his ship destroyed and most of the crew killed or horribly wounded, remain calm, provide leadership, and take care of his sailors?

Figure 72.
Lieutenant Commander Samuel G. Fuqua.

Fuqua was an inspiration to all who saw him that day; men commented on how his coolness inspired them and how they listened to his every instruction, even in the chaos that was the USS *Arizona*. His ship had blown up around him and was burning furiously; dead lay everywhere and horribly burned and wounded men begged for assistance. Many men's lives were saved because of his actions that day. On 11 September there were numerous instances of Americans dealing with disaster and trying to bring order from chaos (Secretary of Defense Donald Rumsfeld went to the site of the Pentagon attack and assisted with casualty evacuation). The staff ride leader should have the students discuss how today's military "makes" leaders who can remain calm in the worst possible scenario and continue to provide leadership to ensure that critical tasks and missions are accomplished.

Stand 10
Japanese Second Wave

Directions: Retrace your route back to the traffic circle and drive ¾ of the way around. Drive southwest on Ford Island Boulevard. After 0.8 miles (when the road starts to bear to the right), turn left into the large parking lot and park at the water's edge.

Orientation: Standing at the southern part of Ford Island. The seaplane ramp and base were just to the southwest where the modern building on the edge of the water now stands. The flagpole and monument across the water are on Hospital Point and mark the USS *Nevada* Memorial. The dry dock where the USS *Pennsylvania*, USS *Downes*, and USS *Cassin* were berthed on 7 December is due east across the loch (there will probably be ships in the dry dock when you are there).

Description: At 0829 the aircraft of the first wave formed up and started back for their carriers, but Fuchida remained to observe the second wave. As he waited, he took stock of the first wave's attack. He had complete control of the air, the *Arizona* was furiously burning, the *Oklahoma* and *Utah* were capsized, the *West Virginia* and *California* were badly damaged and sinking, and some other smaller ships were damaged. Fuchida had only had eight planes go down, but 52 were damaged. At 0840 Fuchida spotted the second wave arriving.

Lieutenant Commander Shigekazu Shimazaki led the second wave, and at 0854 he ordered the attack. The plan for the second wave was considerably different from the first wave. There were no torpedo bombers in the second wave because the planners considered their use too risky without the element of surprise. The dive bombers and high-level bombers changed missions; the high-level bombers attacked the airfields, and the dive bombers attacked the ships in Pearl Harbor. For the second wave, the Japanese had 54 Kate high-level bombers armed with two 550-pound bombs (some had combinations of 550 pound and 132 pound bombs), 78 Val dive bombers armed with a 550-pound bomb, and 35 Zero fighters.

The aircraft of the second wave started their attack by hitting the airfields again. Nine Kates and 18 Zeros attacked Kaneohe at 0900, and when they departed, 33 of the 36 assigned PBYs were destroyed or badly damaged (three PBYs were on patrol during the attack). Nine of the Zeros attacked Bellows Field when they were finished at Kaneohe and destroyed 10 of the 21 planes there. The other nine Zeros headed to strafe Wheeler, but the Army Air Forces had planes in the air now, and six P-40s jumped

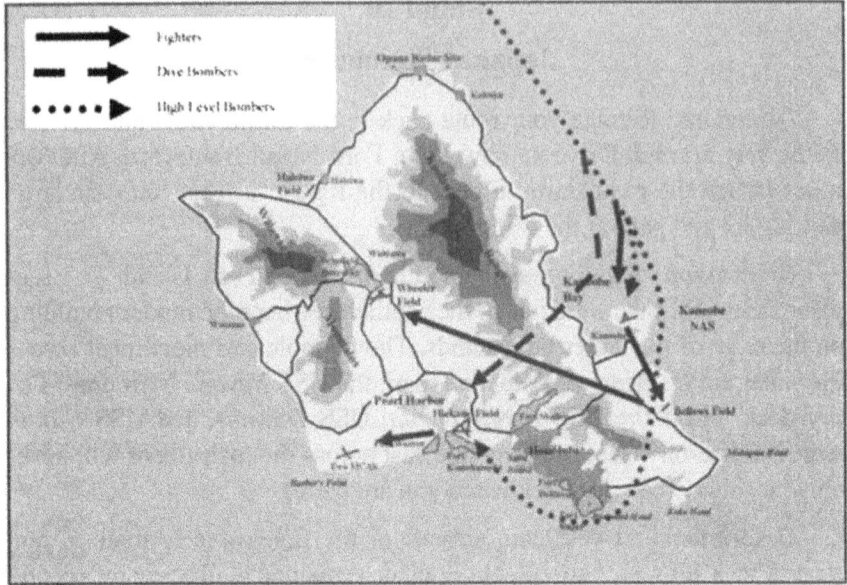

Figure 73. Second-wave plan.

the Zeros heading for Wheeler, destroying four of them and dispersing the rest. Twenty-seven Kates and 18 Zeros attacked Hickam AAF during the second wave, and when they departed, 18 aircraft were destroyed and many more were damaged. Many of the facilities at Hickam were destroyed and damaged. Ewa Field was not a specific target for the second wave but was the location where the Japanese airplanes would rendezvous before heading back to the carriers. Many planes, while waiting for the others, strafed the field, and 33 of the 51 assigned aircraft were destroyed or seriously damaged. Nine Kates continued the attack on Ford Island NAS, and by the end of the day, 26 of the 35 assigned PBYs were destroyed or damaged, as well as many of the hangars and other facilities.

At 0900 the Val dive bombers arrived over Pearl Harbor and started to attack ships. Near misses near the cruisers *St Louis* and *Honolulu*, the destroyers *Cummings* and *Helm*, and the repair ship *Regal* caused different degrees of damage to these ships. In Dry Dock 1, the USS *Pennsylvania* was berthed aft of destroyers USS *Cassin* and USS *Downes*. One bomb hit the *Pennsylvania*, causing minor damage and killing 15 men, but that was the only damage that ship suffered. The *Cassin* was hit twice and the *Downes* was hit once (these may have been bombs aimed at the *Pennsylvania*), which started massive fires. In an effort to extinguish the fires, the dry dock was flooded, causing the *Cassin* to fall over onto the *Downes* and destroying both ships.

The USS *Raleigh* was trying to prevent capsizing from the torpedo hits sustained during the first wave when a dive bomber hit it during the second wave, causing serious damage. A Val was shot down after releasing its bomb at the USS *Curtiss*, a seaplane tender. Both the bomb and the plane hit the *Curtiss* and caused extensive damage. The USS *Shaw*, a destroyer in floating Dry Dock 2, was hit by three bombs, starting an immense fire. The fire ignited the forward magazine, blowing off the bow of the ship and causing a massive explosion that was seen all over Pearl Harbor. Miraculously, the *Shaw* did not sink.

Figure 74. The USS *Cassin* resting on the USS *Downes* after the attack. The USS *Pennsylvania* is in the foreground.

Figure 75. The USS *Shaw* explodes on 7 December.

In port, ships kept one boiler lit to provide power for electricity for the ship. The USS *Nevada* was switching boilers the morning of 7 December, and by 0850 it had enough power from the two boilers to get under way. It backed out of its berth aft of the blazing *Arizona* and dashed to get out of the harbor to search for the Japanese fleet. The Japanese dive bomber pilots spotted the *Nevada* and concentrated their attack on it, hoping to sink it in the harbor's channel so the harbor would be blocked. Five bombs crashed into the *Nevada*, causing fires and extensive damage. Fearful of it sinking, the Naval District ordered the *Nevada* to beach itself at Hospital Point. Against the protests of the crew that wanted to find the Japanese, the *Nevada* beached just after 0900 (at the spot marked by the flag across the water).

Figure 76. The USS *Nevada* on fire and trying to head to sea. Picture taken just north of where you are standing.

At 1000 the second wave formed up and headed back to the carriers. The second wave was not nearly as successful as the first wave, destroying only three destroyers and damaging some other ships. The Japanese had lost six Zeros and 14 Vals and had 16 Kates, 41 Vals, and eight Zeros damaged. When Fuchida landed on his carrier, he debriefed his commanders and tallied the attack. He believed he had sunk five battleships and damaged four more, and he also thought he had destroyed or seriously damaged three cruisers and four destroyers. He did not know specifically how many aircraft his crews had destroyed, but he knew he had control of the skies. He had lost five Kates, 15 Vals, and nine Zeros, and 34 Kates, 58 Vals, and 19 Zeros were damaged.

With reports in hand, Fuchida went to see Commander Minoru Genda, the 1st Air Fleet Air Staff Officer, and Vice Admiral Chuichi Nagumo, the commander. He presented his information and recommended another attack on Pearl Harbor's ships and facilities. Once his briefing was complete, he was dismissed, and Genda and Nagumo considered another strike. Genda recommended staying in the area and launching another strike in the morning, using the night to plan and repair aircraft. However, Nagumo was concerned for his fleet. He remembered what happened during the exercise in September when US planes located his carriers and "sank" one because he lingered in the area. He also did not know the location of the American carriers and was concerned that some of his fleet's smaller ships were low on fuel. Additionally, Nagumo had accomplished his mission, and not one of his ships had suffered a scratch. Nagumo made his decision; he ordered the fleet to set sail for home.

Vignette: On 31 December Rear Admiral Patrick Bellinger, Commander, Patrol Wing 2 (Task Force 9, et al.), expressed his surprise that the Japanese did not return for another attack: "I talked to Admiral Kimmel on the telephone on Sunday about noon, I think, and I said to him then I expected another attack at any time . . . they would refuel and come back; and as they didn't do that—I don't know why because they had a great opportunity." (*IPHA*, part 22, 584.)

Admiral Kimmel gave his assessment of what would have happened if the Japanese had destroyed the fleet's oil tanks and facilities: "if there had not been a ship in port, they could have done serious damage, and if they destroyed the oil which was all above ground at the time and which could have been destroyed, it would have forced the withdrawal of the fleet to the coast because there wasn't any oil anywhere else out there to keep the fleet operating . . . if they had destroyed the base and the facilities in the base and destroyed the oil there it might have been even worse than it was." (*IPHA*, part 6, 2,812.)

Teaching point. Culmination. Did Nagumo miss an opportunity for a decisive victory by not attacking a third time, or did he accomplish his mission?

Again, this is an opportunity in which the staff ride leader can play "devil's advocate." Let the students discuss this for a little while, and if the group is leaning toward Nagumo striking again, remind them:

- The fleet's destroyers and cruisers were very low on fuel.
- One hundred eleven (111) airplanes had been damaged.
- The mission was accomplished; the US Pacific Fleet was crippled for six months.

If the group says Nagumo was right for leaving, remind them:
- Japan had air superiority.
- The fuel tanks and facilities were large area targets that required minimal planning.
- The chance to locate and sink a US carrier was there, and Nagumo had six carriers.

Stand 11
Aftermath

Directions: The staff ride leader has numerous options on where to conduct this stand (the USS *Arizona* Memorial or USS *Missouri* Memorial). The Park Service "may" allow a special trip for military groups (you have to be in uniform) to the USS *Arizona* Memorial at the end of the day, but it must be coordinated well in advance. The Navy also allows military groups to go to the memorial during nonvisiting hours, but this must be coordinated with the Navy well in advance, too.

To get to the USS *Arizona* Memorial, return to Ford Island Boulevard, drive northeast, and leave the island over the bridge. At the traffic light, turn right onto Highway 99 (Kamehameha Highway). At the next light, turn right and park (parking is very crowded here). Conduct the stand down by the water before entering the USS *Arizona* Memorial Visitor's Center where there is a museum, bookstore, and the entrance to where you get on the boat to visit the USS *Arizona* Memorial.

To get to the USS *Missouri* Memorial, return to Ford Island Boulevard and drive northeast. At the traffic circle, go 90 degrees and turn onto Saratoga Boulevard. Follow Saratoga Boulevard and the signs to the USS *Missouri*. There is an entrance fee but there is a military discount. You can conduct the stand on the ship at any place overlooking Pearl Harbor or at the Surrender Plaque on board.

Orientation: If conducted at the water at the USS *Arizona* Memorial Visitor's Center: Standing at the USS *Arizona* Memorial Visitor's Center. The USS *Arizona* Memorial is across the water on Battleship Row on Ford Island. The Navy yard where the USS *Pennsylvania*, USS *Shaw*, etc., were berthed is to the southwest.

If conducted on the USS *Missouri* overlooking Pearl Harbor: Standing on the deck of the USS *Missouri*. The USS *Arizona* Memorial is just northeast. The Navy yard where the USS *Pennsylvania*, USS *Shaw*, etc., were berthed is to the southeast. Ford Island is to the west. Hospital Point is to the south.

Description: The US Pacific Fleet was devastated by the Japanese attack. Four battleships were sunk—the *Arizona, Oklahoma, West Virginia,* and *California*—three battleships were damaged—the *Nevada, Maryland,* and *Tennessee*—four other ships were sunk—the *Utah, Cassin, Downes,* and *Oglala*—and nine others were damaged—the *Honolulu, Helena, St Louis, Raleigh, Vestal, Curtiss, Shaw, Cummings,* and *Helm*. Additionally, other ships, like the *Pennsylvania*, suffered minor damage, and some facilities (Floating Dry Dock 2 and Dry Dock 1) were destroyed or badly damaged. The Army Air Forces lost 165 aircraft and their airfields were a shambles. More than 2,400 servicemen died that day, and another 1,178 were wounded. The civilians of Oahu also suffered casualties; 68 were killed and 35 were wounded. Foretelling 11 September, the Honolulu Fire Department responded to the fires on Hickam AAF; three civilian firefighters were killed in the raid and six were injured.

The services immediately started cleaning up from the attack, and the primary priority became generating combat power for any eventuality. The Navy immediately started repairing its ships. The *Pennsylvania, Tennessee*, and *Maryland* were quickly repaired and returned to the fleet on 20 December 1941. The *Nevada* was refloated and entered Dry Dock 2 on 12 February 1942 where repairs were made so it could sail to the West Coast. It departed Pearl Harbor on 15 March 1942 for Puget Sound Naval Station where it was completely repaired and modernized. The *Nevada* rejoined the fleet in December 1942 and participated in the Aleutians Campaign, the Normandy invasion, the invasion of Southern France, Iwo Jima, and Okinawa.

The *West Virginia* was raised on 17 May 1942 and moved to Dry Dock 1 where temporary repairs were made. It took almost 1 year to make enough temporary repairs for it to sail to the West Coast, but it departed under its own power in April 1943 for Puget Sound where it was fixed and modernized. On 4 July 1944 the *West Virginia* returned to the fleet and participated in numerous campaigns in the Pacific. It was present in Tokyo Bay on 2 September 1945 when the Japanese surrendered. The *California* was raised on 24 March 1942 and entered Dry Dock 2 for repairs. It departed Pearl Harbor for Puget Sound on 10 October 1942 and was returned to the fleet in September 1943. It earned seven battle stars in the Pacific during the war.

The *Shaw*, whose entire bow had been blown off, was fitted with a temporary bow, sailed to the West Coast, and returned to the fleet in October 1943. The *Cassin* and *Downes* were destroyed, but serviceable equipment and machinery were removed from the ships and placed in newly constructed destroyers with the same names, so the *Cassin* and *Downes* "returned" to the fleet. The *Raleigh, Honolulu, Helena, St Louis, Vestal, Curtiss, Oglala, Cummings*, and *Helm* were all repaired and returned to the fleet.

Only three ships that were in Pearl Harbor on 7 December 1941 never returned to the fleet. The *Oklahoma* was a total loss, and in March 1943 the Navy used 21 electric winches on Ford Island to right her. It was decommissioned on 1 September 1944 and sold for scrap for $46,000. On 17 May 1947, while being towed to the West Coast, the *Oklahoma* sank during a storm 500 miles northeast of Hawaii.

Figure 77. Twenty-one winches right the USS *Oklahoma*.

Once the *Oklahoma* was righted, the Navy moved the winches to the other side of Ford Island to use on the *Utah*. Because the *Utah* was only a target ship, the Navy decided to just temporarily roll it out of the shipping lane and salvage it later. In 1950, when the Navy realized that the *Utah* would never be salvaged, the Navy placed a plaque on it to honor the men still entombed in it. On 27 May 1972 the government dedicated the USS *Utah* Memorial in honor of the ship and its brave crew. Each day the Navy raises the American flag at the memorial as a tribute to the 58 men who are still entombed there.

In July 1942 the Navy conducted a survey on the *Arizona* and decided it could not be salvaged. An attempt was made to remove the dead, but after recovering about 100 bodies, the effort was abandoned. The superstructure was removed, and the guns from turrets three and four were removed and given to the Army to use in Coast Artillery batteries (one battery was completed and one was under construction when the war ended). On 1 December 1942 the *Arizona* was stricken from the list of commissioned ships. In 1950, Admiral Arthur Radford, Commander, Pacific Fleet, ordered that the American flag be flown from the *Arizona* and that a small platform be built. In 1958 the US Congress approved a bill that authorized the construction of a memorial, and after raising the required funds, the USS *Arizona* Memorial was dedicated on Memorial Day 1962. Today, the memorial commemorates all the men who died during the attack on 7 December 1941.

On 16 December 1941 Admiral Kimmel and Lieutenant General Short were relieved of their commands. They were never court-martialed, but they did appear before eight official government investigations of the attack, one of which blamed them for "dereliction of duty." For the rest of their lives, these two men tried to clear their names.

The 30 ships that comprised the Japanese fleet that went to Hawaii returned to Japan. By the end of the war, all but one had been sunk; a tanker was the sole survivor. The architect of the plan, Admiral Isoroku Yamamoto, was killed on 18 April 1943 when his aircraft was shot down by US Army planes that learned his location from code breakers. Vice Admiral Chuichi Nagumo, who commanded the 1st Air Fleet on 7 December 1941, killed himself on Saipan on 7 July 1944, two days before the island's capture by US troops. Minoru Genda, the air staff officer who planned the attack, and Mitsuo Fuchida, air commander, both survived the war. Genda entered politics, and Fuchida became a Christian evangelist.

Vignette: Admiral Yamamoto, on being told of the success of the attack on Pearl Harbor, reportedly replied: "We have awakened a sleeping giant and instilled in him a terrible resolve." After the attacks of 11 September 2001, President George W. Bush reported to Congress the feeling of the nation—the same feeling the nation had after Pearl Harbor: "Tonight we are a country awakened to danger and called to defend freedom. Our grief has turned to anger and anger to resolution. Whether we bring our enemies to justice or bring justice to our enemies, justice will be done." (President George W. Bush, address to Congress, 20 September 2001.)

Discussion point: The staff ride leader should tell the students to think about what they have contemplated, thought about, and learned during the staff ride. Have them take some time by themselves for self-reflection and deliberation before gathering for the integration phase.

IV. Integration Phase for the Attack on Pearl Harbor

The integration phase is the most important phase, and no staff ride is complete without it. The integration phase allows students to understand what happened, why it happened, and most important, what can be learned from studying the battle. Integration is the "so what" of the staff ride. The staff ride leader should give the students sufficient time for self-reflection and thought before bringing them together for the integration phase.

The staff ride leader has numerous options on how to conduct the integration phase, but the most important thing is that the students should do most of the talking. One technique is to run the integration phase similarly to a military after-action review: consider what happened, why it happened, and how to fix what was broken. Another technique is to let the students freely express what thoughts they have in their mind after their period of self-reflection. Once a student provides a topic, the staff ride leader can keep the discussion going to get every bit of learning out of each topic.

On 11 September 2001 the United States was again a victim of a surprise attack that damaged the nation and thrust it into a global war. Are there comparisons between 11 September and 7 December? In *The 9/11 Commission Report*, Pearl Harbor is mentioned five times in the conclusion chapter. The similarities are startling and worthy of study and discussion to prevent anything like it from ever happening to the nation again.

As you conduct the integration phase, judge the people and judge their actions, but do so with compassion. The 9/11 Commission cautioned in its conclusion that it was writing with the benefit of hindsight and quoted Roberta Wohlstetter, who in her book *Pearl Harbor: Warning and Decision* wrote, "it is much easier after the event to sort the relevant from the irrelevant signals. After the event, of course, a signal is always crystal clear; we can see what disaster it was signaling since the disaster has occurred. But before the event it is obscure and pregnant with conflicting meanings." The following are possible topics to discuss during the integration phase of the Attack on Pearl Harbor Staff Ride.

Intelligence. Intelligence was arguably the most significant factor in the failures of Pearl Harbor and on 11 September. There are a few areas of intelligence the staff ride leader can explore:

    a. How can we best gather information about our possible enemies? There were many agencies collecting information on Japan before the attack on Pearl Harbor. The Army and Navy were each intercepting different Japanese codes, both diplomatic and military. Many different agencies knew Japanese agents were conducting espionage on Oahu and worked to prevent it. Before 11 September there were at least 14 different agencies gathering information on al-Qaeda. As the 9/11 Commission pointed out, each agency concentrated on its specialized mission. The problem, both in 1941 and in 2001, was that there was no one agency responsible for synchronizing the efforts and analyzing all the information from the varied sources. The 9/11 Commission recommended: "The current position of Director Central Intelligence should be replaced by a National Intelligence Director with two main areas of responsibility: (1) to oversee national intelligence centers on specific subjects of interest across U.S. government and (2) to manage the national intelligence program and oversee the agencies that contribute to it." Ask the students if this is the answer. Have them discuss the advantages and disadvantages of this recommendation.

b. What good is having intelligence if you cannot share it with your subordinate commanders? Before Pearl Harbor, the United States had very good information on Japan's intentions through "Magic," but the list of people cleared to see Magic was extremely limited. The 9/11 Commission observed that the US agencies before 11 September also had good information but were again reluctant to share it. Means and sources need to be protected, but how do we exploit the excellent intelligence that we gather? The 9/11 Commission recommended: "Information procedures should provide incentives for sharing, to restore better balance between security and shared knowledge." Ask the students if this is a realistic solution and if it isn't, how do we get intelligence to the commanders who need it.

Joint. How does the United States best organize itself to detect threats and prepare to deal with an enemy? In Hawaii before the attack on Pearl Harbor there were many agencies that needed to work together to accomplish the mission, "To hold Oahu as a main outlying naval base, and to control and protect shipping in the Coastal Zone." The Army and Navy needed to work together to accomplish this, and within each of the services, subordinate organizations needed to work together. The Army had ground forces, air forces, AA forces, and coast artillery forces, and the Navy had the fleet, the district, air forces, and marines. There was no order that required all the services and organizations to work together; instead, they relied on their professionalism to work toward the common goal.

The 9/11 Commission found problems with interagency coordination that hindered our ability to defend against al-Qaeda. Players included the CIA, FBI, Department of Defense, and Department of State. Now this list also includes the Department of Homeland Security. The commission went on to mention three reasons for joint action: the virtue of joint planning, unity of command, and to simplify the shortage of experts with sufficient skills. The third reason, the shortage of experts, has been a problem since before Pearl Harbor. Recall how long it took the limited number of code breakers to decipher a message and how long it took the limited number of linguists to translate the message. To defend against a terrorist threat on the United States, the 9/11 Commission recommended: "We recommend the establishment of a National Counterterrorism Center (NCTC), built on the foundation of the existing Terrorist Threat Integration Center (TTIC). Breaking the older mold of national government organization, this NCTC should be a center for joint operational planning *and* joint intelligence, staffed by personnel from the various agencies."

Have students discuss if this goes far enough into solving the joint and interagency problems. If not, what needs to be done? The US Northern Command was established in 2002 with the mission to "Conduct operations to deter, prevent, and defeat threats and aggression aimed at the United States . . . provide military assistance to civil authorities." The Department of Homeland Security was also created in 2002 with the mission to " prevent and deter terrorist attacks and protect against and respond to threats and hazards to the nation." Ask students how critical it is for these two agencies to work together.

Prioritization. How should the United States set defensive priorities for the global war on terrorism? The forces in Hawaii in 1941 were not the priority for the United States. The ongoing campaign in the Atlantic was the Navy's and Army's main concern, and the forces in the Philippines had priority over Hawaii. Ask students if US leaders had set the correct priorities in 1941. The 9/11 Commission identifies that the Department of Homeland Security now has to set priorities in allocating limited resources. The commission recommended: "Homeland security assistance should be based strictly on an assessment of risks and vulnerabilities. Now, in 2004, Washington D.C. and New York City are certainly at the top of any such list. . . . It should supplement state and local resources based on the risks and vulnerabilities that merit additional support. Congress should not use this money as a pork barrel." Ask students if this is realistic in this day and age. Also ask them what the best way to prioritize limited resources is. Ask them how units can best prepare if they are not the priority.

Travel. Is it too easy for the United States' enemies to freely travel within its boundaries? Japanese spies assigned to the consulate in Honolulu were free to roam around the country to gather information on military installations and assets, and there was no way to stop them because they were not breaking the law. Before the 11 September attacks, the terrorists were also free to roam around the country to gather information and to prepare for their attack. The 9/11 Commission recommended: "Targeting travel is at least as powerful of a weapon against terrorists as targeting their money. The United States should combine terrorist travel intelligence, operations and law enforcement in a strategy to intercept terrorists, find terrorist travel facilitators, and constrain terrorist mobility." Ask students how best to prevent foreign nationals who have legally entered this country from being able to freely move around to conduct operations against us.

Civil liberties versus security. How do we protect our nation and our civil liberties simultaneously? The very laws that keep us free also make us less secure in our own homeland. Counterespionage agents were prevented from gathering critical information on Japanese spies by such laws as the Federal Communications Act of 1934, which prohibited messages to and from a foreign country from being intercepted. In the aftermath of 11 September, Congress passed the Patriot Act that gave more power to investigative agencies of the government but many fear erodes our civil liberties. As some powers of the Patriot Act are scheduled to expire, the 9/11 Commission recommended: "The burden of proof for retaining a particular government power should be on the executive, to explain (a) that the power actually materially enhances security and (b) that there is adequate supervision of the executive's use of the powers to ensure protection of civil liberties. If the power is granted, there must be adequate guidelines and oversight to properly confine its use." Ask students if the loss of certain civil liberties is worth it if it makes the nation safer. Also ask them if they feel the country trusts its government enough to have these powers.

Vulnerability. How do we mitigate the vulnerability of our facilities and assets? Both the installations on Oahu and the assets and targets on 11 September were vulnerable. Information was easy to obtain because maps and photos were easy to acquire. Organizations became predictable, and unchanging security measures were overcome. Ask the students how the military can mitigate the inherent vulnerabilities of its installations and assets. Areas that students should consider include periodic, randomly scheduled changes to security precautions and constantly changing schedules and timetables to be unpredictable.

Early warning. How do we ensure that people report possible attacks, no matter how improbable they seem? On 7 December the United States had at least two incidents in which the attackers' intentions were shown. In each case, the American personnel involved concluded that there was no possible way that an attack was under way. On 11 September we again had some early warning, and even after airplanes started crashing into buildings, some people could not believe that we were under attack. Have the students discuss how we can ensure personnel report things, no matter how improbable, to the proper authorities. Is the "zero defect" mentality part of the problem? Are people afraid they will be accused of "crying wolf?"

Failures. In what areas did the United States fail before 7 December and 11 September? The 9/11 Commission found four types of failures before the 11 September attack that were also failures before 7 December: imagination, policy, capabilities, and management. The commission believed the United States failed because it did not have the imagination to understand the dangers and did not listen to those who imagined the "impossible." It believed that the United States must make the exercise of imagination routine. Ask the students how well we listen to those who imagine what could happen.

The commission believed that the nation's weak policies toward al-Qaeda were a major failing, just as before December 1941 the nation let Japan get away with actions that went against its policies. Ask the students if weakness and weak policies endanger the nation. Before 11 September the nation had opportunities to destroy al-Qaeda command and control cells, but it did not have the ability to do so (we tried with missiles). Ask the students if preemptive strikes are ever a possibility for the United States. Finally, the commission reported that failures in management helped result in the 11 September attacks. Different agencies did not share information and had conflicting and dissimilar missions. Recall the different missions of the Army and Navy in Hawaii in 1941. Ask the students how management can assist in defending the nation.

Battle command. Was it justifiable to lay the blame for Pearl Harbor on Kimmel and Short? The staff ride leader should consider saving this topic for the end because many different opinions will be expressed. Consider Short and Kimmel not being on the Magic distribution list, the numerous messages and warnings they received and the ones they did not receive, the actions they took before the attack (joint planning or exercises), their reactions to different warnings, and their communications with Washington. This is a great opportunity for students to discuss leadership and responsibility.

V. Support for a Staff Ride to Pearl Harbor

1. Information and assistance. This staff ride was designed primarily for military groups, but with modifications and extensive coordination, civilian organizations can use it as well.

   a. The Staff Ride Team, Combat Studies Institute (CSI), Fort Leavenworth, Kansas, has conducted Pearl Harbor staff rides and can provide advice and assistance on every aspect of the staff ride. The Staff Ride Team can also provide staff ride facilitators to lead a Pearl Harbor staff ride. Visit the CSI Web site for information on obtaining staff ride assistance and/or leadership. Staff Ride Team support includes background information, detailed knowledge of the battle and battlefield, and familiarity with Pearl Harbor and surrounding areas.

   Address: Combat Studies Institute
   US Army Combined Arms Center
   ATZL-CSH
   201 Sedgwick Avenue
   Fort Leavenworth, KS 66027

   Telephone: DSN 552-2078
   Commercial (913) 684-2078

   Web site: <http://usacac.army.mil/CAC/CSI/staff_ride/staffridehome.asp>

   b. Most of this staff ride occurs on active military bases—Naval Station Pearl Harbor and Hickam Air Force Base. In this time of increased security and awareness, it is imperative to coordinate with each installation's military police. Staff ride leaders can take a few steps to make the Pearl Harbor staff ride easier:

   (1) Use military vehicles or privately owned vehicles with Department of Defense stickers (registered on base/post).

   (2) Every member of the staff ride needs to carry his or her military identification so he or she can enter the installations.

   (3) Coordinate at least one working day before with each installation's military police:

   (a) Naval Station Pearl Harbor:
   NAVSTA Pearl Harbor Security Office
   370 Fuller Way
   Pearl Harbor, HI 96860
   (808) 474-6755

(b) Hickam Air Force Base:
15th Security Forces Squadron
505 Hanger Ave
Hickam AFB, HI 96853
(808) 449-2392

b. The National Park Service, which maintains the USS *Arizona* Memorial, can provide advice and assistance to any group desiring to visit the USS *Arizona*. The Visitor's Center includes a small museum with a film on the battle, a bookstore, and restrooms. The Park Service does not usually coordinate special trips to the *Arizona*, and lines can be up to 3 hours. However, the Park Service may be willing to arrange a special visit for military groups in uniform. Coordinate with the memorial's headquarters well before your visit.

Address: 1. Arizona Memorial Place
Honolulu, HI 96818

Telephone: (808) 422-2771, ext 125

Web site: <http://www.nps.gov/usar/>

2. Logistics.

a. Meals. There are many fast food restaurants on Pearl Harbor and Hickam AFB, but these may be crowded during meal times. Groups may consider packing a lunch and eating at one of the base parks.

b. Lodging. Each base has limited on-base lodging. The US military runs the Hale Koa Hotel, a resort on Waikiki, which accepts service members who are TDY. The phone number is 1-800-367-6027, or e-mail is <http://www.halekoa.com>.

c. Medical. Each base has a hospital and clinics that are well marked.

3. Other considerations.

a. Most of this staff ride is on active duty military installations. Staff Ride leaders should be extremely careful not to venture into off-limits areas. Prior reconnaissance of the route is imperative for a successful staff ride.

b. Ensure every member of the group has water. Additionally, some rest rooms are available on the route, but this should be a consideration.

Appendix A
Order of Battle, Japanese Forces

1st Air Fleet: Vice Admiral Chuichi Nagumo

1st Carrier Division: Vice Admiral Chuichi Nagumo
Akagi: Captain Hasegawa Kiichi
Kaga: Captain Okada Jisaku

2d Carrier Division: Rear Admiral Yamaguchi Tamon
Soryu: Captain Yanagimoto Ryusaku
Hiryu: Captain Kaku Tomeo

5th Carrier Division: Rear Admiral Hara Chuichi
Zuikaku: Captain Yokokawa Ichibei
Shokaku: Captain Jojima Takatsugu

Support Force: Vice Admiral Mikawa Gunichi

3d Battleship Division: Vice Admiral Mikawa Gunichi
Hiei: Captain Nishida Masuo
Kirishma: Captain Yamaguchi Jihei

8th Cruiser Division: Captain Komura Keizo
Chikuma: Captain Komura Keizo
Tone: Captain Okada Tarueji

1st Destroyer Squadron: Rear Admiral Omori Sentaro
Abukuma: Captain Murayama Seitoku
Akigumo: Commander Arimoto Terumichi

17th Destroyer Division: Commander Orita Tsuneo
Hamakaze: Commander Orita Tsuneo
Isokaze: Commander Toyoshima Shunichi
Tanikaze: Commander Katsumi Motoi
Urakaze: Commander Shiraishi Nagayoshi

18th Destroyer Division: Commander Ogata Tomie
Arare: Commander Ogata Tomie
Kagero: Commander Yokoi Minoru
Kasumi: Commander Tomura Kiyoshi
Shiranuhi: Commander Akazawa Shizuo

Supply Group 1: Captain Oto Masanao
Kyokuto Maru: Captain Oto Masanao
Kanemasu Maru: Captain Kanemasu Yoshio
Kokuyu Maru: Captain Hidai Toraji
Shinkoku Maru: Captain Ito Tokutaka

Supply Group 2: Captain Niimi Kazutaka
Toho Maru: Captain Niimi Kazutaka
Nippon Maru: Captain Ueda Konoskae
Toei Maru: Captain Kusakawa Kiyoshi

Submarine Patrol Formation: Captain Imaizumi Kijiro
I-19: Commander Narahara Shogo
I-21: Commander Matsumura Kanji
I-23: Commander Shibata Genichi

1st Submarine Group: Rear Admiral Tsutome Sato
I-9: Commander Fujii Akiyoshi
I-15: Commander Ishikawa Nobuo
I-17: Commander Nishino Kozo
I-25: Commander Tayami Meiji

2d Submarine Group: Rear Admiral Yamazaki Shigeaki
I-1: Lieutenant Commander Sakamoto Eichi
I-2: Commander Inoida Hiroshi
I-3: Commander Tonosuka Kinzo
I-4: Commander Nakagawa Hajme
I-5: Commander Shichiji Tsuneo
I-6: Commander Inaba Michimune
I-7: Commander Koizumi Ki'ichi

3d Submarine Group: Rear Admiral Miwa Shigeyoshi
I-8: Commander Emi Tetsushiro
I-68: Commander Nakamuro Otoji
I-69: Commander Watanabe Katsuji
I-70: Commander Sano Takahi
I-71: Commander Kawasaki Mutsuo
I-72: Commander Togami Ichiro
I-73: Commander Isobe Akira
I-74: Commander Ikezawa Masayuki
I-75: Commander Inoue Chikanori

Special Attack Force (Midget Submarine Carriers): Commander Yamada Kaoru
I-16: Commander Yamada Kaoru
I-18: Commander Otani Kiyonori
I-20: Commander Yasuda Takashi
I-22: Commander Agata Kiyo
I-24: Commander Hanabasa Hiroshi

Carrier Air Group: Commander Fuchida Mitsuo

1st Attack Force: Commander Fuchida Mitsuo

1st Group (high-level and torpedo bombers): Commander Fuchida Mitsuo

(High-level bombers carried an 800-kilogram [KG] bomb.)
(Torpedo bombers carried an 800 KG torpedo.)

1st Attack Unit: Commander Fuchida Mitsuo (15 Kates from the *Akagi*)

2d Attack Unit: Commander Hashiguchi Takashi (15* Kates from the *Kaga*)

3d Attack Unit: Lieutenant Abe Heijiro (10 Kates from the *Soryu*)

4th Attack Unit: Lieutenant Commander Kusumi Tadashi (10 Kates from the *Hiryu*)

1st Torpedo Attack Unit: Lieutenant Commander Murata Shigeharu (12 Kates from the A*kagi*) (Shigeharu was the torpedo plane leader.)

2d Torpedo Attack Unit: Lieutenant Kitajima Ichiryo (12 Kates from the *Kaga*)

3d Torpedo Attack Unit: Lieutenant Nagai Tsuyoshi (8 Kates from the *Soryu*)

4th Torpedo Attack Unit: Lieutenant Matsumura Heita (8 Kates from the *Hiryu*)

2d Group (dive bombers): Lieutenant Commander Takahashi Kakuchui

(Dive bombers carried a 250 KG bomb.)

15th Attack Unit: Lieutenant Commander Takahashi Kakuchui (27* Vals from the *Shokaku*)

16th Attack Unit: Lieutenant Ema Tomatsu (27** Vals from the *Zuikaku*)

3d Group (fighters): Lieutenant Commander Itaya Shigeru

1st Fighter Combat Unit: Lieutenant Shiga Yoshio (9 Zeros from the *Kaga*)

2d Fighter Combat Unit: Lieutenant Commander Itaya Shigeru (9 Zeros from the *Akagi*)

3d Fighter Combat Unit: Lieutenant Suganami Masaharu (9* Zeros from the *Soryu*)

4th Fighter Combat Unit: Lieutenant Okajima Kiyokuma (6 Zeros from the *Hiryu*)

5th Fighter Combat Unit: Lieutenant Kaneko Tadashi (6* Zeros from the *Shokaku*)

6th Fighter Combat Unit: Lieutenant Sato Masxao (6 Zeros from the *Zuikaku*)

2d Attack Force: Lieutenant Commander Shimazaki Shigekazu

1st Group (high-level bombers): Lieutenant Commander Shimazaki Shigekazu

(High-level bombers carried either two 250 KG bombs or 1 250 KG bomb and six 60 KG bombs.)

5th Attack Unit: Lieutenant Ichihara Tatsuo (27 Kates from the *Shokaku*)

6th Attack Unit: Lieutenant Commander Shimazaki Shigekazu (27 Kates from the *Zuikaku*)

2d Group (dive bomber): Lieutenant Commander Egusa Takehige

(Dive bombers carried a 250 KG bomb.)

11th Attack Unit: Lieutenant Chihaya Takehiko (18 Vals from the *Akagi*)

12th Attack Unit: Lieutenant Makino Saburo (27* Vals from the *Kaga*)

13th Attack Unit: Lieutenant Commander Egusa Takehige (18* Vals from the *Soryu*)

14th Attack Unit: Lieutenant Kobayashi Michio (18* Vals from the *Hiryu*)

3d Group (fighters): Lieutenant Shindo Saburo

1st Fighter Combat Unit: Lieutenant Shindo Saburo (9 Zeros from the *Akagi*)

2d Fighter Combat Unit: Lieutenant Nikaido Yasushi (9 Zeros from the *Kaga*)

3d Fighter Combat Unit: Lieutenant Iida Fusata (9 Zeros from the *Soryu*)

4th Fighter Combat Unit: Lieutenant Nono Sumio (9* Zeros from the *Hiryu*)

* One aircraft aborted/crashed during takeoff.
** Two aircraft aborted during takeoff.

Aircraft Compilation
(Number of Aircraft Planned/Number of Aircraft Launched)

1st Attack Force

	Kate	Kate High-Level	Val Torpedo	Zero
Akagi	15/15	12/12		9/9
Kaga	15/14	12/12		9/9
Soryu	10/10	8/8		9/8
Hiryu	10/10	8/8		6/6
Shokaku			27/26	6/5
Zuikaku			27/25	6/6
Subtotal	50/49	40/40	54/51	45/43

1st Attack Force total   189/183

2d Attack Force

	Kate High-Level	Val	Zero
Akagi		18/18	9/9
Kaga		27/26	9/9
Soryu		18/17	9/9
Hiryu		18/17	9/8
Shokaku	27/27		
Zuikaku	27/27		
Subtotal	54/54	81/78	36/35

2d Attack Force total   <u>171/167</u>

Carrier Air Group Total   360/350

Appendix B
Order of Battle, US Forces

US Navy

US Pacific Fleet: Admiral Husband E. Kimmel

On 7 December 1941 there were 207 ships in the Pacific Fleet, organized into three main task forces. There were 103 ships in Pearl Harbor that morning, and the other 104 ships were out to sea. Following are the ships that were in Pearl Harbor on 7 December 1941:

Battle Force (Task Force 1)
Vice Admiral William S. Pye

Battleships, Battle Force
Rear Admiral Walter S. Anderson

Battleship Division 1
Rear Admiral Isaac C. Kidd
BB-36 *Nevada* (Nevada class)—Captain Francis W. Scanland
BB-38 *Pennsylvania* (Pennsylvania class)—Captain Charles M. "Saavy" Cooke, Jr.
BB-39 *Arizona* (Pennsylvania class)—Captain Franklin Van Valkenburg

Battleship Division 2
RADM D.W. Bagley
BB-37 *Oklahoma* (Nevada class)—Captain Howard D. "Ping" Bode
BB-43 *Tennessee* (Tennessee class)—Captain C. E. Reordan
BB-44 *California* (Tennessee class)—Captain Joel W. Bunkley

Battleship Division 4
RADM Walter S. Anderson
BB-46 *Maryland* (Colorado class)—Captain D.C. Godwin
BB-48 *West Virginia* (Colorado class)—Captain Mervyn Bennion

Cruisers, Battle Force
Rear Admiral H. Fairfax Leary

Cruiser Division 6 (Partial)
CA-32 *New Orleans* (New Orleans class)—J.G. Atkins
CA-38 *San Francisco* (New Orleans class)—D.J. Callaghan

Cruiser Division 9
Rear Admiral H. Fairfax Leary
CL-46 *Phoenix* (Brooklyn class)—H.E. Fischer
CL-48 *Honolulu* (Brooklyn class)—H. Dodd

CL-49 *St. Louis* (St. Louis class)—G.A. Rood
CL-50 *Helena* (St. Louis class)—R.H. English

Destroyers, Battle Force
Rear Admiral Milo F. Draemel

Destroyer Flotilla 1
CL-7 *Raleigh* (Omaha class)—R.B. Simons

Destroyer Squadron One
DD-360 *Phelps* (Porter class)—E.L. Beck

Destroyer Division One
DD-349 *Dewey* (Farragut class)—A.J. Detzer
DD-350 *Hull* (Farragut class)—R.F. Stout
DD-351 *MacDonough* (Farragut class)—J. M. McIsaac
DD-352 *Worden* (Farragut class)—W.C. Pogue

Destroyer Division Two
DD-348 *Farragut* (Farragut class)—G.P. Hunter
DD-353 *Dale* (Farragut class)—A.L. Rorschach
DD-354 *Monaghan* (Farragut class)—W.P. Burford
DD-355 *Aylwin* (Farragut class)—R.H. Rodgers

Destroyer Squadron Three
DD-357 *Selfridge* (Porter class)—W. Craig

Destroyer Division Five
DD-369 *Reid* (Mahan class)—H.F. Pullen
DD-371 *Conyngham* (Mahan class)—H.C. Daniels
DD-372 *Cassin* (Mahan class)—D.F. Shea
DD-375 *Downes* (Mahan class)—W.R. Thayer

Destroyer Division Six
DD-365 *Cummings* (Mahan class)—G.D. Cooper
DD-370 *Case* (Mahan class)—R. W. Bedilion
DD-373 *Shaw* (Mahan class)—W. Glenn Jones
DD-374 *Tucker* (Mahan class)—W.R. Terrlell

Destroyer Flotilla 2
CL-8 *Detroit* (Omaha class)—L.J. Wiltse

DD-386 *Bagley* (Bagley class)—G.A. Sinclair
DD-387 *Blue* (Bagley class)—H.N. Williams
DD-388 *Helm* (Bagley class)—C.E. Carroll
DD-389 *Mugford* (Bagley class)—E.W. Young
DD-390 *Ralph Talbot* (Bagley class)—R. Earle, Jr.

DD-391 *Henley* (Bagley class)—R.H. Smith
DD-392 *Patterson* (Bagley class)—F.R. Walker
DD-393 *Jarvis* (Bagley class)—J.R. Topper

Other Destroyers

DD-66 *Allen* (Sampson class)—D.B. Miller
DD-103 *Schley* (Wickes class)
DD-106 *Chew* (Wickes class)—H.R. Hummer, Jr.
DD-139 *Ward* (Wickes class)—W.W. Outerbridge

Submarines

SS-167 *Narwhal*—G.W. Wilkins
SS-169 *Dolphin*—G.B. Rainer
SS-170 *Cachalot*—W.N. Christensen
SS-199 *Tautog*—J.H. Willingham, Jr.

Minelayer

CM-4 *Oglala*—E.P. Speight

Minesweepers

AM-13 *Turkey*—T.F. Fowler
AM-20 *Bobolink*—J.L. Foley
AM-26 *Rail*—F.W. Beard
AM-31 *Tern*—W.B. Pendleton
AM-43 *Grebe*
AM-52 *Vireo*—F.J. Ilsemann

Coastal Minesweepers

AMC-8 *Cockatoo*
AMC-9 *Crossbill*
AMC-14 *Condor*
AMC-30 *Reedbird*

Destroyer Minelayers

DM-15 *Gamble*—D.A. Crandell
DM-16 *Ramsay*—G.C. Simms
DM-17 *Montgomery*—R.A. Guthrie
DM-18 *Breese*—H.F. Stout
DM-19 *Tracy*—G.R. Phelan
DM-20 *Preble*—H.D. Johnston
DM-21 *Sicard*—W.C. Shultz
DM-22 *Pruitt*—E.W. Herron

Destroyer Minesweepers

DMS-14 *Zane*—L.M. LeHardy
DMS-15 *Wasmuth*—J.L. Wilfong
DMS-16 *Trever*—D.M. Agnew
DMS-17 *Perry*—L.H. Miller

Patrol Gunboat

PG-19 *Sacramento*—A.L. Warburton

Destroyer Tenders

AD-3 *Dobbin*—H.E. Paddock
AD-4 *Whitney*—N.M. Pigman

Seaplane Tenders

AV-4 *Curtiss*—H.S. Kendall
AV-8 *Tangier*—C.A. Sprague

Small Seaplane Tenders

AVP-4 *Avocet*—W.C. Johnson, Jr.
AVP-7 *Swan*—F.E. Hall

Seaplane Tenders (Converted Destroyer)

AVD-6 *Hulbert*—J.M. Lane
AVD-11 *Thornton*—W.F. Kline

Ammunition Ship

AE-1 *Pyro*—N. Vytacil

Oilers

AO-12 *Ramapo*—D. Curry, Jr.
AO-23 *Neosho*—J.S. Phillips

Repair Ships

AR-1 *Medusa*—A.E. Schrader
AR-4 *Vestal*—C. Young
AR-11 *Rigel*—R. Dudley

Submarine Tender

AS-14 *Pelias*—W. Wakefield

Submarine Rescue Ship

ASR-1 *Widgeon*—J.A. Flenniken

Hospital Ship
   AH-5 *Solace*—B. Perlman
Cargo Ship
   AK-17 *Vega* (at Honolulu)
Stores Issue Ships
   AKS-1 *Castor*—H.J. Wright
   AKS-3 *Antares*—L.C. Grannis
Ocean Tugs
   AT-13 *Ontario*—E.C. Mayer
   AT-28 *Sunnadin*
   AT-38 *Keosanqua*
   AT-64 *Navajo* (12 miles outside the Pearl Harbor entrance)
Miscellaneous Auxiliaries
   AG-16 *Utah* (target ship)—J.M. Steele
   AG-31 *Argonne*—F.W. Connor
   AG-32 *Sumner*—I.M. Truitt
   CM-1 (ex C-3) *Baltimore* (out of commission)

14th Naval District: Rear Admiral Claude C. Bloch

Commander, Hawaiian Patrol Wing (also Commander, Task Force 9): Rear Admiral Patrick N.L. Bellinger

US Marine Corps

   Marine Air Group 1: Lieutenant Colonel Claude A. Larkin (Ewa MCAS)
      VMB-232
      VMJ-252
      VMF-211 (rear echelon)
      VMB-231 (rear echelon)

   Marine Barracks, Pearl Harbor: COL Gilder D. Jackson
      1st Defense Battalion (-)
      2d Engineer Battalion
      3d Defense Battalion
      4th Defense Battalion
      Company A(-), 2d Service Battalion

Sixteen ships (eight battleships, two heavy cruisers, four light cruisers, and two auxiliaries) had US Marine Corps detachments embarked.

US Army

Hawaiian Department: LTG Walter C. Short (Fort Shafter)

24th Division: BG Durward S. Wilson (Schofield Barracks)
25th Division: MG Maxwell Murray (Schofield Barracks)
Hawaiian Coast Artillery Command: MG Henry T. Burgin (Fort Ruger)
Hawaiian Army Air Force: MG Frederick L. Martin (Hickam Field)
18th Bombardment Wing: BG J.H. Rudolph (Hickam Field)
14th Pursuit Wing : BG H.C. Davidson (Wheeler Field)

Appendix C
Biographical Sketches

US Leaders and Commanders

Franklin Delano Roosevelt—President of the United States. Roosevelt was born 30 January 1882 in Hyde Park, New York, the fifth cousin of President Theodore Roosevelt. He graduated from Harvard in 1903 with a degree in history before studying law at Columbia University. He passed the bar before graduating from law school and never earned his law degree. In 1910 he entered local politics as a Democrat. There he earned the attention of Woodrow Wilson, who appointed him as Assistant Secretary of the Navy in 1913. In 1920 he was the Democratic nominee for vice president for James. M. Cox, but when Warren G. Harding won the election, Roosevelt returned to private life. In 1921 he contracted polio, and despite his valiant efforts, he lost the use of his legs. In 1928 Roosevelt returned to public life, being elected governor of New York and reelected in 1930.

In 1932 he was elected President of the United States. Roosevelt's aggressive actions helped bring the nation out of the Great Depression, and he was reelected in 1936 and 1940. Roosevelt wanted the United States to be neutral in the war that had started in Europe, but actions like the Lend-Lease Act allied the United States with the French and British (et al.). Roosevelt became a wartime president on 8 December 1941. After calling the Japanese attack "a date which will live in infamy," he asked Congress for its approval and declared war. Roosevelt led the nation as it continued to mobilize and slowly enter the war. Roosevelt was elected to a fourth term in 1944. The Allies had almost won the war when, on 12 April 1945, Roosevelt suffered a stroke and died at Warm Springs, Georgia. He is buried at his family estate in Hyde Park, New York.

George C. Marshall—Chief of Staff, US Army. Marshall was born on 31 December 1880 in Uniontown, Pennsylvania. He attended the Virginia Military Institute and graduated in 1901 as the Senior First Captain of Cadets. Commissioned in the infantry, Marshall served on numerous posts in the United States and Philippines before attending the Army Staff College in 1908. Marshall was appointed to the General Staff and served during World War I, where many noticed his achievements. After the war, he served in continuingly significant positions. He served as aide de camp to General John. J. Pershing; was an instructor at the US Army War College; commanded the 8th Infantry Regiment; and after promotion to brigadier general, commanded the 5th Infantry Brigade. In 1938 Marshall was posted to the General Staff in Washington, where he was appointed as Chief of Staff, US Army in 1939. He was Chief of Staff on 7 December 1941 but received no blame for the attack. During World War II, he supervised the training, armament, and mobilization of 8 million soldiers. When the war ended, Marshall retired, but President Truman asked him to again serve, first as an envoy to China, and then as Secretary of State from 1947-49. As Secretary of State, he developed a plan for Europe's economic recovery that was named after him. He served as Secretary of Defense in 1950-51 before retiring for good. In 1953 he was awarded the Nobel Prize for the Marshall Plan. Marshall died in Walter Reed Hospital on 16 October 1959 and is buried in Arlington National Cemetery.

Harold R. Stark—Chief of Naval Operations. Starke was born on 12 November 1880 in Wilkes-Barre, Pennsylvania. He graduated from the US Naval Academy at Annapolis in 1903. His initial service included tours on the battleship *Minnesota*, followed by duty with torpedo boats and destroyers. During World War I, Starke served on the staff of the Commander, US Naval Forces Europe. After the war, Starke served as the executive officer on two battleships, attended the Naval War College, and commanded an ammunition ship. Promoted to captain, he commanded the battleship *West Virginia*, Cruiser Division 3, and Battle Force cruisers. Starke had made friends with Roosevelt when Roosevelt was the Assistant Secretary of the Navy, and Starke was appointed as Chief of Naval Operations in 1939. After Pearl Harbor, Starke was replaced as the Chief of Naval Operations and assigned to the 12th Fleet in England, where he oversaw preparations for and executed the landings at Normandy in 1944. He retired in 1946 and died on 21 August 1972 at his home in Washington, DC.

Husband E. Kimmel—Commander, Pacific Fleet. Kimmel was born in Henderson, Kentucky on 26 February 1882. Upon graduation from the US Naval Academy, Kimmel served on numerous ships, including battleships, and in 1933 he commanded the battleship *New York*. In November 1937 Kimmel was promoted to vice admiral and became Commander, Cruiser Division 7. In 1939 he was commander, Battle Force Cruisers. In February 1941 Kimmel was selected over 32 officers to replace Admiral James Richardson as Commander, Pacific Fleet. Kimmel was relieved of command on 16 December 1941, but he was allowed to retire in March 1942. Kimmel was never court-martialed but was found lacking by numerous commissions that investigated the attacks. Kimmel spent the rest of his life trying to clear his name. He died at Groton, Connecticut on 14 May 1958.

Walter C. Short—Commander, Hawaiian Department. Short was born on 30 March 1880 in Fillmore, Illinois. He graduated from the University of Illinois in 1902 and received a direct commission in the infantry. His early postings were to Texas, the Presidio of San Francisco, the Philippines, and Alaska. He served with the 16th Infantry during the punitive expedition in Mexico. During World War I he observed French and British troops and then organized training for Americans. After the war he went to the Army School of the Line, Fort Leavenworth, Kansas and was also an instructor at Leavenworth. He commanded the 1st Infantry Division and I Corps. He assumed command of the Hawaiian Department on 7 February 1941. He was relieved of his command on 16 December 1941 and allowed to retire in March 1942. Short took a job with the Ford Motor Company. He died on 3 September 1949 and was buried with full military honors in Arlington National Cemetery. Only his wife, son, daughter-in-law, and a few close friends attended.

Japanese Leaders and Commanders

Hideki Tojo—Prime Minister. Tojo was born in Tokyo on 30 December 1884, the son of an army general. He graduated from the Japanese Military Academy in 1905. In 1915 he graduated from the war college and went to work in the mobilization section of the War Ministry where he developed his thoughts on total war as a doctrine for Japan. Tojo wanted to reorganize the army and wanted Japan to expand its borders. Tojo served in China as Chief of Police Affairs and Chief of Staff of the army in China. He was appointed Vice Minister of War in 1938 and Minister of War in 1940. As Minister of War, his mobilization plans increased tensions between Japan and the United States. On 16 October 1941 Tojo became premier when the government was broken up. He was the Prime Minister of Japan as well War Minister and Army Chief of Staff, which basically made him Japan's dictator. He remained in this position until he resigned on 19 July 1944 because of serious setbacks in the war. After Japan surrendered, Tojo attempted suicide by shooting himself in the chest, but American doctors saved his life. The International Military Tribunal found him guilty of war crimes, and he was hanged in Tokyo on 23 December 1948.

Isoroku Yamamoto—Commander, Combined Fleet. Yamamoto was born on 4 April 1884, adopted by the Yamamoto family, and took their name. He graduated from the Japanese Military Academy in 1904 and was assigned as an ensign on a cruiser during the Battle of Tshushima in 1905, where he was wounded and lost two fingers. After recovering from his wound, he continued his naval career and continued to progress. From 1919-21 Yamamoto studied in the United States at Harvard. In 1923 Yamamoto was commander of the air training base at Kasumiguara, where he became an aviation advocate. In 1926 he started a two-year tour as the naval attaché in Washington, and in 1930 he was the Japanese navy's representative to the London Naval Conference. While head of Japanese naval aviation, Yamamoto championed aviation and was instrumental in developing the Zero fighter and torpedo attack doctrine. He commanded an aircraft carrier division from 1933-35, where he impressed many and was then appointed as Vice Minister of the Navy. In 1939 Yamamoto was named Commander, Combined Fleet. Yamamoto opposed war with the United States, but when war became inevitable, he oversaw the Pearl Harbor attack plan. In June 1942 Yamamoto led the Combined Fleet at Midway where he lost four aircraft carriers. In April 1943 US intelligence personnel decoded Japanese radio traffic and learned that Yamamoto was flying to the Solomon Islands for an inspection. The Army Air Forces organized an attack, and on 18 April 1943 shot down Yamamoto's plane, killing him.

Chuichi Nagumo—Commander, 1st Air Fleet. Nagumo was born in Northern Honshu on 25 March 1887. He graduated from the Japanese Military Academy in 1908 followed by service on battleships, cruisers, and destroyers. After a teaching assignment at the Naval Staff College, he was promoted to captain and given command of a light cruiser followed by command of a destroyer division. In 1934 he commanded the battleship *Yamashiro*. Nagumo was promoted to admiral, and at the start of World War II, he became Commander, 3d Battleship Division. In 1939 he was promoted to vice admiral and served as President of the Naval Staff College. When Japan formed the 1st Air Fleet, Nagumo was given command based mainly on seniority and despite his lack of aviation experience. Nagumo led the 1st Air Fleet as it prepared for and executed the attack on Pearl Harbor. Nagumo survived the Battle of Midway but lost his command when the United States sank four Japanese carriers. Nagumo was given minor commands after Midway, including command of a backwater fleet in Vietnam. In July 1944 Nagumo was the commander of the naval detachment on Saipan. On 7 July 1944, just two days before the island fell to the Americans, Nagumo killed himself.

Minoru Genda—Air Staff Officer, 1st Air Fleet. Genda was born on 16 August 1904 in Hiroshima. He graduated from the Japanese Military Academy with his friend Fuchida in 1924. He graduated from flight training and became a fighter pilot, earning a reputation as the best fighter pilot in the Japanese navy. He also commanded an aerobatic group named "Genda's Flying Circus" that flew demonstrations all around Japan. His operational assignments included tours on the carriers *Ryujo* and *Akagi*, combat duty in China, and instructor duty at flight school. While Genda attended the staff college, he wrote extensively on carrier-based air power, and his controversial thoughts alienated him from many of his peers. He was the assistant naval attaché in London during the blitz. He was appointed as the Air Staff Officer, 1st Air Fleet in February 1941 and was the primary planner for the attack on Pearl Harbor. Genda remained in this post until the Battle of Midway cost the Japanese the carriers of the 1st Air Fleet. Genda became the senior air staff officer of the General Staff and remained in this post until December 1944 when Japan formed Air Group 343, the most experienced pilots flying the best aircraft, which Genda led until the end of the war. From 1959-62 Genda served as the Chief of Staff, Japanese Air Force. When he retired from the air force, Genda entered politics and served in Parliament until 1986. He died in Tokyo on 15 August 1989, one day short of his 85th birthday.

Mitsuo Fuchida—Air Group Commander, 1st Air Fleet. Fuchida was born on 2 December 1902. In 1921 he entered the Japanese Military Academy where be became friends with Genda. Fuchida fell in love with flying while at the academy and entered flight school in 1927. Fuchida was the Japanese "ace" of high-level bombing and taught it at the flight school. He wrote extensively on air tactics while attending the Naval Staff College. In 1939 he was the flight commander of the *Akagi* where he met Yamamoto, whom he greatly respected. Fuchida next was the Air Officer, 3d Carrier Division, but he was soon recalled to the *Akagi* for combat action in China. In August 1941 he was named Commander, Air Group, 1st Air Fleet. In this position he supervised the training and led the attack on Pearl Harbor. During Midway, Fuchida was recovering from appendicitis and could not lead any flights. He was badly injured while evacuating the sinking *Akagi*. Fuchida convalesced until June 1943, and during this time, he wrote analyses of major battles, including Coral Sea and Midway. In June 1943 he joined the staff of the now land-based 1st Air Fleet. For the rest of the war, Fuchida served as an air staff officer, coordinating the land-based Japanese naval air arm. After Japan's surrender, Fuchida converted to Christianity and became an evangelist. He wrote of his wartime service and was interviewed numerous times about Pearl Harbor. He died 30 May 1976.

Appendix D
Medal of Honor Conferrals for the Attack on Pearl Harbor

The United States awarded 15 Medals of Honor, 51 Navy Crosses, five Distinguished Service Crosses, and 69 Silver Stars in recognition of valorous service during the attack on Pearl Harbor. The following are the names of and citations for the Medals of Honor earned on 7 December 1941. Asterisks indicate posthumous awards.

*Bennion, Mervyn Sharp. Rank and organization: Captain, US Navy. Born: 5 May 1887, Vernon, UT. Appointed from Utah. Citation: For conspicuous devotion to duty, extraordinary courage, and complete disregard of his own life, above and beyond the call of duty, during the attack on the Fleet in Pearl Harbor by Japanese forces on 7 December 1941. As Commanding Officer of the USS *West Virginia*, after being mortally wounded, Captain Bennion evidenced apparent concern only in fighting and saving his ship and strongly protested against being carried from the bridge.

Finn, John William. Rank and organization: Lieutenant, US Navy. Place and date: Naval Air Station, Kaneohe Bay, territory of Hawaii, 7 December 1941. Entered service in California. Born: 23 July 1909, Los Angeles, CA. Citation: For extraordinary heroism, distinguished service, and devotion above and beyond the call of duty. During the first attack by Japanese airplanes on the Naval Air Station, Kaneohe Bay, on 7 December 1941, Lieutenant Finn promptly secured and manned a .50-caliber machine gun mounted on an instruction stand in a completely exposed section of the parking ramp, which was under heavy enemy machine gun strafing fire. Although painfully wounded many times, he continued to man this gun and to return the enemy's fire vigorously and with telling effect throughout the enemy strafing and bombing attacks and with complete disregard for his own personal safety. It was only by specific orders that he was persuaded to leave his post to seek medical attention. Following first aid treatment, although obviously suffering much pain and moving with great difficulty, he returned to the squadron area and actively supervised the rearming of returning planes. His extraordinary heroism and conduct in this action were in keeping with the highest traditions of the US Naval Service.

*Flaherty, Francis C. Rank and organization: Ensign, US Naval Reserve. Born: 15 March 1919, Charlotte, MI. Accredited to Michigan. Citation: For conspicuous devotion to duty and extraordinary courage and complete disregard of his own life, above and beyond the call of duty, during the attack on the Fleet in Pearl Harbor by Japanese forces on 7 December

1941. When it was seen that the USS *Oklahoma* was going to capsize and the order was given to abandon ship, Ensign Flaherty remained in a turret, holding a flashlight so the remainder of the turret crew could see to escape, thereby sacrificing his own life.

Fuqua, Samuel Glenn. Rank and organization: Lieutenant Commander (LCDR), US Navy, USS *Arizona*. Place and date: Pearl Harbor, territory of Hawaii, 7 December 1941. Entered service in Laddonia, MO. Born: 15 October 1899, Laddonia, MO. Citation: For distinguished conduct in action, outstanding heroism, and utter disregard of his own safety above and beyond the call of duty during the attack on the Fleet in Pearl Harbor, by Japanese forces on 7 December 1941. Upon the commencement of the attack, LCDR Fuqua rushed to the quarterdeck of the USS *Arizona* to which he was attached where he was stunned and knocked down by the explosion of a large bomb which hit the quarterdeck, penetrated several decks, and started a severe fire. Upon regaining consciousness, he began to direct the fighting of the fire and the rescue of wounded and injured personnel. Almost immediately there was a tremendous explosion forward, which made the ship appear to rise out of the water, shudder, and settle down by the bow rapidly. The whole forward part of the ship was enveloped in flames which were spreading rapidly, and wounded and burned men were pouring out of the ship to the quarterdeck. Despite these conditions, his harrowing experience, and severe enemy bombing and strafing, at the time, LCDR Fuqua continued to direct the fighting of fires to check them while the wounded and burned could be taken from the ship and supervised the rescue of these men in such an amazingly calm and cool manner and with such excellent judgment that it inspired everyone who saw him and undoubtedly resulted in the saving of many lives. After realizing the ship could not be saved and that he was the senior surviving officer aboard, he directed it to be abandoned but continued to remain on the quarterdeck and directed abandoning ship and rescue of personnel until satisfied that all personnel that could be had been saved, after which he left his ship with the last boatload. The conduct of LCDR Fuqua was not only in keeping with the highest traditions of the US Naval Service but characterizes him as an outstanding leader of men.

*Hill, Edwin Joseph. Rank and organization: Chief Boatswain, US Navy. Born: 4 October 1894, Philadelphia, PA. Accredited to Pennsylvania. Citation: For distinguished conduct in the line of his profession, extraordinary courage, and disregard of his own safety during the attack on the Fleet in Pearl Harbor by Japanese forces on 7 December 1941. During the height of the strafing and bombing, Chief Boatswain Hill led his men of the line handling details of the USS *Nevada* to the quays, cast off the lines, and swam back to his ship. Later, while on the forecastle, attempting to let go the anchors, he was blown overboard and killed by the explosion of several bombs.

*Jones, Herbert Charpoit. Rank and organization: Ensign, US Naval Reserve. Born: 1 December 1918, Los Angeles, CA. Accredited to California. Citation: For conspicuous devotion to duty, extraordinary courage, and complete disregard of his own life, above and beyond the call of duty, during the attack on the Fleet in Pearl Harbor by Japanese forces on 7 December 1941. Ensign Jones organized and led a party, which was supplying ammunition to the antiaircraft battery of the USS *California*, after the mechanical hoists were put out of action when he was fatally wounded by a bomb explosion. When two men attempted to take him from the area which was on fire, he refused to let them do so, saying in words to the effect, "Leave me alone! I am done for. Get out of here before the magazines go off."

*Kidd, Isaac Campbell. Rank and organization: Rear Admiral, US Navy. Born: 26 March 1884, Cleveland, OH. Appointed from Ohio. Citation: For conspicuous devotion to duty, extraordinary courage, and complete disregard of his own life, during the attack on the Fleet in Pearl Harbor by Japanese forces on 7 December 1941. Rear Admiral Kidd immediately went to the bridge and, as Commander, Battleship Division One, courageously discharged his duties as Senior Officer Present Afloat until the USS *Arizona*, his flagship, blew up from magazine explosions and a direct bomb hit on the bridge which resulted in the loss of his life.

Pharris, Jackson Charles. Rank and organization: Lieutenant, US Navy, USS *California*. Place and date: Pearl Harbor, territory of Hawaii, 7 December 1941. Entered service in California. Born: 26 June 1912, Columbus, GA. Citation: For conspicuous gallantry and intrepidity at the risk of his life above and beyond the call of duty while attached to the USS *California* during the surprise enemy Japanese aerial attack on Pearl Harbor, territory of Hawaii, 7 December 1941. In charge of the ordnance repair party on the third deck when the first Japanese torpedo struck almost directly under his station, Lieutenant (then Gunner) Pharris was stunned and severely injured by the concussion that hurled him to the overhead and back to the deck. Quickly recovering, he acted on his own initiative to set up a hand-supply ammunition train for the antiaircraft guns. With water and oil rushing in where the port bulkhead had been torn up from the deck, with many of the remaining crewmembers overcome by oil fumes, and the ship without power and listing heavily to port as a result of a second torpedo hit, Lieutenant Pharris ordered the shipfitters to counterflood. Twice rendered unconscious by the nauseous fumes and handicapped by his painful injuries, he persisted in his desperate efforts to speed up the supply of ammunition and at the same time repeatedly risked his life to enter flooding compartments and drag to safety unconscious shipmates who were gradually being submerged in oil. By his inspiring leadership, his valiant efforts and his extreme loyalty to his ship and its crew, he saved many of his shipmates from death and was largely responsible for keeping the *California* in action during the attack. His heroic conduct throughout this first eventful engagement of World War II reflects the highest credit upon Lieutenant Pharris and enhances the finest traditions of the US Naval Service.

*Reeves, Thomas James. Rank and organization: Radio Electrician (Warrant Officer), US Navy. Born: 9 December 1895, Thomaston, CT. Accredited to Connecticut. Citation: For distinguished conduct in the line of his profession, extraordinary courage, and disregard of his own safety during the attack on the Fleet in Pearl Harbor by Japanese forces on 7 December 1941. After the mechanized ammunition hoists were put out of action on the USS *California*, Reeves, on his own initiative, in a burning passageway, assisted in the maintenance of an ammunition supply by hand to the antiaircraft guns until he was overcome by smoke and fire, which resulted in his death.

Ross, Donald Kirby. Rank and organization: Machinist, US Navy, USS *Nevada*. Place and date: Pearl Harbor, territory of Hawaii, 7 December 1941. Entered service in Denver, CO. Born: 8 December 1910, Beverly, KS. Citation: For distinguished conduct in the line of his profession, extraordinary courage, and disregard of his own life during the attack on the Fleet in Pearl Harbor, territory of Hawaii, by Japanese forces on 7 December 1941. When his station in the forward dynamo room of the USS *Nevada* became almost untenable due to smoke, steam, and heat, Machinist Ross forced his men to leave that station and performed all the duties himself until blinded and unconscious. Upon being rescued and resuscitated, he returned and secured the forward dynamo room and proceeded to the after dynamo room where he was later again rendered unconscious by exhaustion. Again recovering consciousness he returned to his station where he remained until directed to abandon it.

*Scott, Robert R. Rank and organization: Machinist's Mate First Class, U.S. Navy. Born: 13 July 1915, Massillon, OH. Accredited to Ohio. Citation: For conspicuous devotion to duty, extraordinary courage, and complete disregard of his own life, above and beyond the call of duty, during the attack on the Fleet in Pearl Harbor by Japanese forces on 7 December 1941. The compartment in the USS *California* in which the air compressor, to which Scott was assigned as his battle station, was flooded as the result of a torpedo hit. The remainder of the personnel evacuated that compartment but Scott refused to leave, saying words to the effect, "This is my station and I will stay and give them air as long as the guns are going."

*Tomich, Peter. Rank and organization: Chief Watertender, US Navy. Born: 3 June 1893, Prolog, Austria. Accredited to New Jersey. Citation: For distinguished conduct in the line of his profession, extraordinary courage, and disregard of his own safety during the attack on the Fleet in Pearl Harbor by the Japanese forces on 7 December 1941. Although realizing that the ship was capsizing as a result of enemy bombing and torpedoing, Tomich remained at his post in the engineering plant of the USS *Utah* until he saw that all boilers were secured and all fire room personnel had left their stations, and by so doing lost his own life.

*Van Valkenburgh, Franklin. Rank and organization: Captain, US Navy. Born: 5 April 1888, Minneapolis, MN. Appointed from Wisconsin. Citation: For conspicuous devotion to duty, extraordinary courage, and complete disregard of his own life during the attack on the Fleet in Pearl Harbor by Japanese forces on 7 December 1941. As commanding officer of the USS *Arizona*, Captain Van Valkenburgh gallantly fought his ship until the USS *Arizona* blew up from magazine explosions and a direct bomb hit on the bridge that resulted in the loss of his life.

*Ward, James Richard. Rank and organization: Seaman First Class, US Navy. Born: 10 September 1921, Springfield, OH. Entered service in Springfield, OH. Citation: For conspicuous devotion to duty, extraordinary courage, and complete disregard of his life, above and beyond the call of duty, during the attack on the Fleet in Pearl Harbor by Japanese forces on 7 December 1941. When it was seen that the USS *Oklahoma* was going to capsize and the order was given to abandon ship, Ward remained in a turret holding a flashlight so the remainder of the turret crew could see to escape, thereby sacrificing his own life.

Young, Cassin. Rank and organization: Commander, US Navy. Born: 6 March 1894, Washington, DC. Appointed from Wisconsin. Other Navy award: Navy Cross. Citation: For distinguished conduct in action, outstanding heroism, and utter disregard of his own safety, above and beyond the call of duty, as commanding officer of the USS *Vestal*, during the attack on the Fleet in Pearl Harbor, territory of Hawaii, by enemy Japanese forces on 7 December 1941. Commander Young proceeded to the bridge and later took personal command of the 3-inch antiaircraft gun. When blown overboard by the blast of the forward magazine explosion of the USS *Arizona*, to which the USS *Vestal* was moored, he swam back to his ship. The entire forward part of the USS *Arizona* was a blazing inferno with oil afire on the water between the two ships; as a result of several bomb hits, the USS *Vestal* was afire in several places, was settling, and taking on a list. Despite severe enemy bombing and strafing at the time and his shocking experience of having been blown overboard, Commander Young, with extreme coolness and calmness, moved his ship to an anchorage distant from the USS *Arizona* and subsequently beached the USS *Vestal* upon determining that such action was required to save his ship.

Another hero from Pearl Harbor was **Mess Attendant Second Class Doris Miller**. Miller was a cook on the USS *West Virginia*, and during the attack, he was assisting the wounded when he was told to assist the mortally wounded captain. After the captain died, Miller manned a machine gun and fired at the Japanese planes. Miller had never fired a machine gun before but was able to hit one of the attacking planes. Miller was the first African-American to be awarded the Navy Cross. Rank and organization: Mess Attendant Second Class, US Navy. Born: 12 October 1919, Waco, TX. Appointed from Texas. Citation: For distinguished devotion to duty, extraordinary courage, and disregard for his own personal safety during the attack on the Fleet in Pearl Harbor, territory of Hawaii, by Japanese forces on 7 December 1941. While at the side of his captain on the bridge, Miller, despite enemy strafing and bombing and in the face of a serious fire, assisted in moving his captain, who had been mortally wounded, to a place of greater safety, and later manned and operated a machine gun directed at enemy Japanese attacking aircraft until ordered to leave the bridge.

Bibliography

While not comprehensive, this bibliography provides a list of publications that will be useful for staff ride preparation.

I. Conducting a Staff Ride

Robertson, William G. *The Staff Ride*. Washington DC: US Army Center of Military History, 1987.

This book is the US Army's "doctrine" for conducting staff rides and offers information on organizing and conducting staff rides.

II. Battle

Barkley, Alben W. *Hearings Before the Joint Committee on the Investigation of the Pearl Harbor Attack*. Washington, DC: US Government Printing Office, 1946.

Between December 1941 and June 1946 the government conducted official inquiries—the Roberts Commission, Hart Inquiry, Army Pearl Harbor Board, Navy Court of Inquiry, Clark Investigation, Clausen Investigation, Hewitt Inquiry—into the Pearl Harbor attack. These investigations gathered numerous valuable documents that the Seventy-Ninth Congress compiled during its investigation. The 40 volumes provide valuable information about the attack.

Burlingame, Burl. *Advance Force Pearl Harbor*. Annapolis, MD: Naval Institute Press, 1992.

A detailed history of the Japanese submarine operations during the attack.

Cohen, Stan. *Attack on Pearl Harbor: A Pictorial History*. Missoula, MT: Pictorial Histories Publishing Co., Inc., 2001.

A superb collection of photos from the attack.

Farago, Ladislas. *The Broken Seal*. New York: Random House, 1967.

An excellent book on "Operation Magic" before the attack.

Goldstein, Donald M. and Katherine V. Dillon, eds. *The Pearl Harbor Papers*. New York: Brassey's, 1993.

A first-rate collection of original Japanese documents about the attack.

Kimmett, Larry and Margaret Regis. *The Attack on Pearl Harbor*. Seattle, WA: Navigator Publishing, 1991.

This oversized paperback, available from the US Park Service Web site, is an outstanding illustrated (many valuable pictures) volume on the attack.

Lambert, John W. and Norman Polmar. *Defenseless: Command Failure at Pearl Harbor*. St. Paul, MN: Motorbooks International, 2003.

This book investigates the culpability of Admiral Kimmel and Lieutenant General Short.

Prange, Gordon W. *At Dawn We Slept*. New York: Penguin Books, 1981.

Arguably, the best single volume for a detailed study of both sides' preparations, the attack, and the aftermath.

Smith, Stanley H., ed. *Investigations of the Attack on Pearl Harbor—Index to Government Hearings*. New York: Greenwood Press, 1990.

Smith's index of the 40 volumes the Seventy-Ninth Congress gathered is a valuable tool in navigating the exhibits of the investigations. See *Hearings Before the Joint Committee on the Investigation of the Pearl Harbor Attack*.

Van Der Vat, Dan. *Pearl Harbor: The Day of Infamy—An Illustrated History*. Toronto: Madison Press Books, 2001.

Another illustrated book on the attack and its aftermath.

Willmott, H.P. *Pearl Harbor*. London: Cassell & Co., 2001.

This is an excellent recent publication that covers the attack from all perspectives. Do not let the coffee table book look deceive you; this is an excellent source.

Wohlstetter, Roberta. *Pearl Harbor: Warning and Decision*. Palo Alto, CA: Stanford University Press, 1962.

This excellent book details all of the warnings the United States had before Pearl Harbor and discusses how it must be able to "filter" the many reports to separate the good from the bad to prevent a future attack.

III. Biographies

Roosevelt

Freidel, Frank. *Franklin D. Roosevelt: A Rendezvous With Destiny*. Boston, MA: Little, Brown, & Co., 1990.

Good biographies of Franklin abound, but this is an excellent one-volume biography.

Kimmel

Beach, Edward L. *Scapegoats: A Defense of Kimmel and Short at Pearl Harbor*. Annapolis, MD: Naval Institute Press, 1995.

A modern-day defense of Kimmel and Short.

Brownlow, Donald G. *The Accused: The Ordeal of Rear Admiral Husband Edward Kimmel, U.S.N*. New York: Vantage, 1968.

A good, general biography of Kimmel.

Kimmel, Husband Edward. *Admiral Kimmel's Story*. Chicago: Regnery, 1955.

Kimmel's defense of his actions concerning the attack.

Short

Anderson, Charles R. *Day of Lightning, Years of Scorn: Walter C. Short and the Attack on Pearl Harbor*. Annapolis, MD: Naval Institute Press, 2004.

A brand new biography on a soldier who has been ignored for too long.

Tojo

Butow, Robert J.C. *Tojo and the Coming of the War*. Palo Alto, CA: Stanford University Press, 1961.

The definitive biography of Tojo.

Yamamoto

Hoyt, Edwin B. *Yamamoto: The Man Who Planned Pearl Harbor*. New York: McGraw-Hill, 1990.

A very good biography of Yamamoto.

Fuchida

Prange, Gordon. *God's Samurai: Lead Pilot at Pearl Harbor*. New York: Brassey's, 1990.

Gordon Prange interviewed Fuchida extensively for his book *At Dawn We Slept*. He wrote this biography based on those interviews.

Other

Kean, Thomas H., chairman. *The 9/11 Commission Report: Final Report of the National Commission on Terrorist Attacks Upon the United States*. New York: W.W. Norton & Co., 2004.

About the Author

Lieutenant Colonel Jeffrey J. "Benny" Gudmens was born in Cincinnati, Ohio. He received a B.A. in history from the University of Dayton and an M.A. in Civil War studies from American Military University. His assignments include platoon leader and company executive officer, 82d Airborne Division; airborne company command, 6th Division; assistant G3 air, XVIII Airborne Corps during Operations DESERT SHIELD/DESERT STORM; observer/controller, Joint Readiness Training Center; battalion operations officer, 5-20 Infantry, Fort Lewis, Washington; operations officer, Battle Command Training Program, Fort Leavenworth, Kansas; and operations adviser to the Royal Saudi Land Forces. He is currently Chief, Staff Ride Team, Combat Studies Institute, US Army Combined Arms Center, Fort Leavenworth, Kansas.

www.ingramcontent.com/pod-product-compliance
Lightning Source LLC
Chambersburg PA
CBHW061800110426
42742CB00012BB/2228